"**The Accidental Hostess** is a work of such n   ...ce, such poignant humor and such biting wit, that to not buy, re   ... use it should be declared a capital felony in the State of Florida, punishable by life in prison."

Marty Arnowitz
Ft. Myers Attorney

"Regardless of your age, health or physical limitations, you can purchase **A.H.** for only $9.95 (or only ten easy payments of $.95 each). There is no medical examination required and this book cannot be repossessed at any time. So take the risk out of entertaining. Remember, you're in good hands with **The Accidental Hostess**."

Bob Ochs
Retired Insurance Executive

"**The Accidental Hostess** is already receiving critical acclaim from coast to coast (San Carlos Bay to the Gulf of Mexico). With this brilliant and sensitive work, Moni, Barb, Betty and Mary are sure to become legends in their own minds."

Verlin Rasmussen
Retired Business Executive

"**The Accidental Hostess** is not only a masterpiece of literature, but an incredible value for your literary dollar. With 46,000 words for only $9.95, you pay only $.0002 per word in after tax dollars with adjustments for appreciation and inflation. An investment opportunity of this scope comes along but once in a lifetime."

Allen Ten Broek
Sanibel and Captiva Businessman

the Accidental Hostess

A light hearted approach to coping with constant company, with recipes for breakfast, lunch, dinner and SURVIVAL

by: Moni Arnowitz
Barb Ochs
Betty Rasmussen
Mary Ten Broek

REQUIRED READING FOR ALL RESORT AREA RESIDENTS!

DEDICATION

We dedicate this book to the residents of Sanibel and Captiva Islands, and to the thousands of visitors who frequent these shores and share our love for this enchanted area. It is also intended for, and we hope will be helpful to residents of other popular vacation destinations. We hope you'll read it, use it, enjoy it and keep it as a memento of our Islands in the Sun. It is written with our special love for this special place. Enjoy!

 # OUR SPECIAL THANKS TO:

Annie Cook: For your invaluable help editing, and for not being too brutally honest.

Klaus Ortmann: For your suggestions and help editing our recipes.

Our husbands, Marty, Bob, Verlin and Allen: For your support, encouragement, and selfless assistance at recipe testing. We love you for it, even with those extra 15 pounds!

Recipe Contributors:

Betty Abbott, Kim Bourdon, Katherine Church, Rose Coppola, Grace Harn, Liz Hunt, Penny Hunt, Priscilla Isaacson, Claire Kleinhans, Jane Lawson, Grace McGinn, Merri Murphy, Bill Ochs, Ellie See, Marty Swats, Nancy Thalstrup, Yvonne Whitmore, Merida Worner, Kate Dietrich.

TABLE OF CONTENTS

ABOUT THE AUTHORS

The original idea for the Accidental Hostess was born on the tennis court. Moni Arnowitz, Barb Ochs and Betty Rasmussen played in a weekly doubles match at the Dunes on Sanibel; but they spent more time looking for substitutes than actually playing tennis, because each of them was constantly coping with out of town company. Over a period of time, their frustration led them to a "someone ought to write a book about this!" attitude, which quickly evolved into a "**WE** OUGHT TO WRITE A BOOK ABOUT THIS!" plan of action. A flurry of meetings convinced them further that they were on to something. Surely other resort area residents, interval owners and short term renters experienced the same influx of seasonal company, and could benefit from their collective experiences and advice. Clearly a book must be written, but by WHOM?

Enter, court left, Mary Ten Broek. I joined the group as a tennis sub and brought with me, a weak backhand, but a strong desire to someday write the Great American Novel.

I'd long considered myself a budding new writer, whose career was definitely going in the right direction, however slowly. I'd progressed nicely through the ranks of obligatory literary stages: grocery lists, notes to the teacher, letters to the editor, and a twenty-five year collection of the Ten Broek family Christmas letters. But I'd been stalled at this soon-to-be-famous stage for many years, and was growing restless. (Sort of like a potential home run slugger who'd been in a temporary batting slump for fifteen years!)

All that changed on that fateful morning in November. Little did any of us realize at the time that our Wednesday morning match of mediocre tennis was, in fact, our rendezvous with destiny!

Conversation quickly revealed that Moni, Barb, and Betty had a great idea in search of an author, and that I was a would-be author in search of a great idea. Our tennis match, however lousy, appeared to be one made in heaven.

Acquaintances evolved into friendships and finally into a partnership. Together we would produce the desperately needed and long overdue survival manual for coping with constant company, **THE ACCIDENTAL HOSTESS!**

We hope the product of our efforts will bring you as much pleasure as the process brought us.

Mary Ten Broek

 INTRODUCTION

This book is the effort of four full-time residents of Sanibel Island, Florida, wives, mothers, homemakers, pink collar workers. Together we are responsible for and accountable to four husbands, six homes, nineteen children, three dogs, two fish, thirteen grandchildren, a lovebird and a rabbit. We are civic minded, politically active and health conscious. We are **FOR** bike paths, Perestroika and oat bran. We are **AGAINST** live shelling, famine and cholesterol. Besides time and our sanity, we try to **SAVE** the Pirate Playhouse, The Children, and the wetlands. We are ordinary women, each living ordinary lives. But, we live in an **EXTRAORDINARY** place, the lovely resort area of Sanibel Island.

Sanibel is a beautiful tropical jewel, kissed by the sun, framed in white sand and caressed by the azure blue waters of the Gulf of Mexico. We all feel it is as close to paradise as we'll ever get, and that's why we live here. It is also, not surprisingly, the vacation destination of zillions of visitors each year.

The tourists come in droves to see the beaches, the wildlife, the sunsets and yes, while they are in town, to see **US!** To those of us who are fortunate enough to live on Sanibel, "THE SEASON" (Christmas through Easter) brings the three "C's": Cars, Crowds and the big "C" word, **COMPANY,** each of which impacts our life style profoundly.

Ah yes, "Company." How many times have each of us answered the phone and heard these five little words? "We are in the area" and "We'd love to see you"! ... pause ... The translation is of course, the five BIG words, "WE EXPECT TO BE ENTERTAINED!"

We all have our favorite house guest horror stories - they come for a bite, stay all night ... come just to peek, stay all week, type! We have each found ourselves playing shell seeker, alligator peeker, and boarding house keeper! And we have certainly all found ourselves at the end of long days (and the beginning of long days, and the middle of long days!) dishing up eats, LOTS AND LOTS OF EATS to the huddled masses of sun seekers who happen to be temporarily living in our homes.

Thus we are prodded into a role we didn't ask for, aren't prepared for and often don't care for. We must play tour guiders and room and board providers. We are the quintessential **ACCIDENTAL HOSTESSES!**

And that's what this book is all about. We have each survived many years on the front lines of accidental hostesshood. We're summa cum laude graduates of the **School of Hard Knock, Knock Knocks!** And we've learned **A LOT!**

We've learned how to differentiate between and to prioritize out-of-town guests. We've learned to dish up meals fit for a king without a major budget sting. And we've learned to survive it all with our sanity, families and friendships still intact. But most of all, we've learned to actually ENJOY it all!

This book is an attempt to share our hard won knowledge, our tricks of the trade. It includes recipes for breakfast, lunch, dinner and SURVIVAL. It is intended to assist and entertain other resort area residents, our fellow ACCIDENTAL HOSTESSES!

Rene Descartes, the father of modern philosophy, proclaimed:

> "Cogito ergo sum."
> "I think, therefore I am."

The Accidental Hostess, the mother of modern hospitality proclaims:

> "Habito ergo de cum"
> "I live here, therefore I entertain."

It is simply a fact of life that to live here, or near any other resort area is to have constant out of town company. Our job is to deal with it.

So we **WILL** be entertaining - but WHO?

In democracies, all men are created equal, but in our homes, all guests are not. They come in a vast array of sizes, shapes and most importantly degrees of desirability. Some are so welcome we do sprills when they pull into our driveway; others are so unwelcome we do sprills when they pull out. So the trick here is to figure out WHO'S WHO? and plan the degree of attention they receive accordingly. We recommend you prioritize your guests and assign them to one of the following categories:

CATEGORY I: FAMILY

Folks in this classification are of course **top priority** and get class A, state of the art service and accommodations. It also sounds like a pretty simple straight forward classification to identify. But watch out, it can be tricky. There are all kinds of "family". "Immediate family" members are, of course easy to spot and qualify for designer treatment. So do folks who are "practically family" or "like family." But watch out for the whole herd of sun lovers who are 32nd cousins - sort of GENERIC RELATIVES. They are not bad people, don't get us wrong - there are just so many of them, it would be wise to downgrade their degree of service category to a II or III.

CATEGORY II: DEAR FRIENDS

This one is easy as long as you remember the cardinal rule of thumb as to who gets into this coveted classification. And the rule is . . . "YOU DECIDE!" Dear ole "what's her name" doesn't qualify. Neither does the gal you met at the ABWA luncheon in 1973 in Corn-on-the-Cob, Ohio, nor does your husband's old fraternity brother from Slippery Rock State, Class of '53. Dear friends - you decide who they are, but be very choosey, for they also deserve your best imitation of the hostess with the mostess.

CATEGORY III: DROP-INS

Now this is a huge and vastly diversified group. It ranges from a friend of your son's old clarinet teacher, to your husband's former boss's ex-wife to your old obstetrician. Because of this diversity, it is essential that you learn quickly to differentiate between those you truly love to see, and the "what's your hurry - here's your hat" crowd. But fear not, we have tricks-a-plenty for this group and with a little practice, you can master them all. (For instance - for your old obstetrician, who isn't any more welcome at the other end of your dining room table than at the other end of his examining table, we've found dropping the word "malpractice" a few times works nicely to shorten the visit.)

CATEGORY IV: SPRING BREAKERS

Now this is an unusual category and not applicable to all of our readers life styles; but we have included it for it is a category with which this writer has had such vast experience that in a court of law she could easily qualify as an "expert witness." For two consecutive years Chez' Ten Broek had 16 spring breakers in residence for ten consecutive days. That's 320 student nights, or **more significantly,** 960 meals! We said "more significantly" regarding meals as we've found Spring Breakers don't always make it back to sleep every night but, without exception, they **NEVER MISS A MEAL!** So for those of you who find yourselves in a similar predicament, read on and take heart - suggestions aplenty await. Also, hints in this section should be helpful to anyone who on occasion informally entertains large groups of guests, be they college students or not. Feeding and housing the huddled masses is never easy but with our guidance and coaching, you can muscle through it.

CATEGORY I

FAMILY:

As we mentioned earlier, it is absolutely essential that you learn to differentiate between "family" and **"FAMILY"**. There are many differences. "Family" are relatives, but distant; **"FAMILY"** are immediate or very close. "Family" are heard from only at reunions and when they're in town; **"FAMILY"** maintain a close relationship, even if you move to Raincloud, Indiana. Most significantly, "family" stay in a motel, but **"FAMILY"** stay with you, as houseguests.

This section deals with **"FAMILY"**. As we recommended earlier, "family" should be downgraded to category II or III, but **"FAMILY"** are top priority and deserve, and will appreciate, your best effort.

Your best effort will need to cover these areas:

    a. Entertainment or activities
    b. Accommodations
    c. Meals

ENTERTAINMENT:

Let's start with entertainment as it's the easiest. Activities abound on this tropical island paradise or any resort area. Between the beaches, the shells, the sun and the Gulf, it's pretty hard to be bored while on Sanibel or Captiva Islands. But here are a few suggestions for diversity, or in case the weather, a sunburn or bug bites keep you from the beach.

- Take a canoe trip through the bird sanctuary or on Tarpon Bay. It's appropriate and fun for all ages with proper supervision. Canoes are readily available for rent. See the yellow pages for details.

- Take a trolley ride. It's cheap, fun and kids love it. A map of trolley stops is available at the Chamber of Commerce.

- Visit the Elementary School "Kidsplay" playground and recreation complex on San Cap Road. The playground is incredible and open to the public during non-school hours.

- Try your hand at the Sanibel Fishing Pier. It's on the bay side of the East end of the Island and a popular hangout for local anglers.

- Go on a charter fishing trip. Large party charter boats are available on nearby Ft. Myers Beach. Small boat charters are available at several island marinas. Check the yellow pages for locations.

- Go bike riding. Sanibel abounds with bike paths and rentals are readily available. Check the yellow pages or local papers.

- Take a nature tour. Many guided tours are available and are a great source of entertainment and information on our local flora and fauna.

- Visit the J. "Ding" Darling National Wildlife Refuge. We recommend either sunrise or sunset trips when the abundance of wildlife in this remarkable sanctuary is most visible.

- Learn to windsurf. It's fun and challenging. There are several fine instructors on the Islands. See the yellow pages for information.

- Visit our local shops. Sanibel and Captiva have hundreds of unique boutiques of every imaginable variety. Local papers are a good source of information.

- Play golf or tennis. Public tennis courts are available at the Elementary School. There are two golf courses on Sanibel. Both are open to the public, but call ahead for information and tee times.

- Rent a video or go to a movie. Both are available on the Islands. The library has educational videos available.

- Visit our art galleries. We have many wonderful local artists and craftsmen, and their work is displayed and available for purchase at several fine local galleries.

- Fly a kite. They are available in local toy shops in infinite variety. If you've never flown a kite on the beach, you've missed one of life's simplest and purest pleasures.

- Visit the library and our local book stores. A great read in the back yard can be a delightful break during a hectic vacation.

- Keep games on hand. That dead period between dinner and bed time can be filled with lively competition.

- Visit the Sanibel Historical Museum, the Big Arts Center and City Hall. They are all located on the beautiful City Hall site between Periwinkle Way and Palm Ridge Road.

- Check out the activities at the Sanibel Community Association. Many daytime and evening events are available.

- Watch the papers for BIG ARTS and local theater events. They are numerous and excellent.

- Enjoy a legendary Sanibel Sunset from the causeway islands. It's a sight we take for granted, but your guests won't soon forget.

- On a breezy day watch the windsurfers from the causeway islands. Southwest Florida is the home of many nationally recognized boardsailors and they all train in this ideal location. As you see them gracefully maneuver their brilliant sails to harness the wind, you'll wonder if you're watching a sport or a ballet.

This list could go on forever and we've left room to add your own ideas or ideas appropriate for your area. It includes activities for all ages, and more importantly, activities your houseguests can enjoy either with you or ON THEIR OWN. Remember, you can't be a hostess, accidental or otherwise, 24 hours a day. Your guests are on vacation but YOU ARE NOT, and you have your own daily activities to maintain. Encourage guests to strike off on their own as much as possible. Arm them with local maps, shell books, newspapers and suggestion lists, and be sure to remind them to make arrangements for a rental car. They'll enjoy the adventure of discovering these wondrous islands on their own as much as you did the first time.

ACCOMMODATIONS:

The accommodations for houseguests are of course, in your home. Sharing your home with others, especially for extended visits, can be tricky. Plan ahead. Our main piece of advice regarding preparing your home is the same as for planning activities:

ENCOURAGE YOUR GUESTS TO BE SELF-SUFFICIENT

They may be here for only a week or so, but they are probably replaced promptly by another, and another and another batch of sun seekers. The cumulative effect of four or five months of back to back company can be scary. (We know of a lady who, after the disembarkation of the annual Easter invasion, put on her old blue terry bathrobe with the torn pocket and grape jelly stain, locked herself in her bedroom for four days, and, it is rumored, did nothing but watch soaps, eat Spaghetti-Os and read Batman comic books.)

Some down time, private time, quiet time for yourself is essential, and the more your guests look after themselves, the more of it you'll have. **SO MAKE IT EASY FOR THEM TO MAKE IT EASY FOR YOU.** Here are some suggestions:

- Put together a Happy Houseguest Handbook such as you find in most hotels or condominiums. It can include local newspapers, maps, restaurant menus, books of local history, wildlife guide books, shell books, babysitter lists, emergency numbers and activity suggestions. It will encourage your guests to learn about the area and plan activities which most interest them.

- Provide guests, either verbally or better yet in writing, with household rules and information. This can include information on where to find clean linens, how to work the washer and dryer, meal hours, where to find cleaning supplies and paper goods, how to work the coffee pot.

- Make it easy for them to take care of their own space. Try:

    - A laundry basket in each room.
    - Plenty of bars to hang damp towels.
    - Bathroom cleaning supplies under each sink.
    - Suggestions on where to store luggage.
    - A foot bath (dish pan and water) and sandy towel box **outside** each entrance. Your guests need to know that "SAND" and "HOME" are both four letter words and are inherently incompatible.

Try posting this sweet little poem:

"VIOLETS ARE BLUE, ROSES ARE RED.
BRING SAND IN THE HOUSE, AND YOU'LL BE DEAD!"

- Provide guests with a survival kit of sunscreen, bug repellent, cortisone cream, etc. Nothing ruins a vacation quicker, or keeps guests in your house longer, than a bad sunburn or no-seeum bites.

- If your houseguests have children, they of course have special needs. But it is possible to peacefully co-exist if you plan carefully. Try a few of these suggestions:

  - Plan sleeping areas carefully, preferably near their parents and away from you.

  - Provide an early morning T.V. watching area, with a pre-set volume.

  - Set out cereal, bowls, and eating rules, the night before. Be sure the milk is on a low shelf.

  - Provide an arts and crafts box. It can contain paper, crayons, glue, scissors, buttons, macaroni, string, paper bags, whatever. Provide a designated area for creativity - probably not the top of the living room coffee table.

  - If you have a yard, provide supplies for tents or forts. (Blankets and broom handles work nicely - so do card tables and sheets.) All kids love forts, not only for play, but naps and picnics also.

  - Provide a beach basket for kids containing flip-flops, buckets and shovels, water toys, etc.

  - Kid proof your home. Valuable or breakable objects, and poisons should be out of reach.

  - Be sure kids know house rules - especially designated eating and play areas.

  - Keep lots of paper plates, cups, etc. on hand. They'll go fast!

If your young houseguests come equipped with parents who look after and discipline them, you are lucky. Some do not. In that case, it's up to you. Remember, it's your house so be fair but firm. It will make the visit more fun for everyone.

And now, with all this free time you have on your hands, because your guests are doing for themselves, here's our next suggestion:

MAKE IT SIMPLE, BUT MAKE IT SPECIAL!

You don't have to do much to make your home look and feel special. Our balmy breezes, rustling palms and sun drenched living areas do much to set the mood for our wonderful Florida indoor-outdoor life style. But there are some little touches you can try which are cheap and easy and will help make your home feel like a lavish tropical resort. Try these suggestions:

- Turn off the A.C. and keep shades, windows, sliders, drapes, etc. open. Remember your guests probably came from an environment of canned, processed air. While visiting, let them enjoy the smell and feel of FRESH.

- Take advantage of our lavish tropical flora. Try corsaging each room with a hibiscus or gardenia (de-ant them first), stems of sea grapes or bougainvilleas, baskets of ferns or small palms. Remember, these things are readily available and commonplace to us, but our guests probably haven't seen live growies for months.

- Take advantage of any and all outdoor entertaining areas you may have. Porches, patios, decks and docks are great, but use your imagination. One of the most memorable evenings this accidental hostess ever spent on the Islands was as the guest of a couple staying in a very small condominium. Since indoor space was limited, we dined outside on card tables, al fresco, under the stars. The fare was simple, but the setting was spectacular. The moon spotlighted the silken water and the stars provided ambient lighting. Soon the Florida Evening Orchestra tuned up. Lapping water, rustling fronds and a chorus of insects and birds joined the light show creating an audio/visual extravaganza. So remember, on these luscious tropical islands you don't have to create the atmosphere - just take advantage of it.

- If you are a music freak, use it in your mood-setting master plan. Let personal taste be your guide but whether your favorite is Classical, New Age, Jimmy Buffett or Reggae, a background of music helps guests enjoy the ambience of the islands.

- Encourage your guests to read by providing good books in each bedroom. There is an abundance of literature available by local writers, as well as famous works written on or about the islands, such as Ann Morrow Lindbergh's **A Gift from**

the Sea. Also, magazines, (such as our favorite, **Islands**,) make for a great late night read. A good light and a stack of literary goodies provide both you and your guests with an evening of peaceful relaxation, Island Style.

■ In general, provide a mood in your home which encourages your guests to experience and enjoy the intrinsic feeling of softness offered by our islands. The beauty of Sanibel and Captiva is not one which screams at you and demands your attention. Rather, it is one which whispers softly, beckons you to come closer, look more carefully, be still and absorb. By setting a compatible mood at home, you can help your guests become aware of this quality - to transform themselves into a subtle receiving mode.

MEALS:

Ah meals! Definitely we've saved the worst for last. Is there a reader among us who doesn't know that the synonym for "entertain" is "cook"... as in "COOK YOUR BRAINS OUT"? Three meals a day, seven days a week, fifty-two weeks a year, times however many mouths you're entertaining... they eat, so you cook.

We heard recently of an Accidental Hostess whose family did a lot of offshore boating, usually with friends aboard, and inevitably the scene was the same. While her husband regaled their guests with his Man-Against-the-Sea routine, she played designated galley wench. This lead to a weird nightmare. In it their boat was surrounded by wild and potentially vicious animals. They kept circling the boat and snarling, but never really harmed her as long as she kept throwing them food. "What," she asked us, "might this dream mean?"

"We think," we compassionately replied, "we better get you out of the galley!"

Even with our own families, but particularly with guests, we get the message loud and clear.

"DISH IT UP, OR DIE!"

But don't panic now - remember you are in the hands of card-carrying experts. We know lots and lots of ways to make the food and beverage department of the Accidental Hostess's Hometel run smoothly, efficiently, and cost effectively.

Let's start with the general and move toward the specific.

Our most important general rule is this:

PREPARE MEALS USING PRIMARILY THE FRESH, LOCAL PRODUCTS THAT ARE SO READILY AVAILABLE IN THIS AREA.

Now this may sound like a keen sense of the obvious to you, but trust us, people forget this. Because wonderful fresh produce and seafoods are so common and available in Florida, we tend to forget what a treat they are to northern visitors. When you want to make meals special for guests, cook the foods they came for, not the foods they came from. This might mean breaking old habits, but you can do it. When we first moved here, our standard "company" meal was PROCESSED Wisconsin cheese, FROZEN Iowa beef, PACKAGED Minnesota wild rice, CANNED Ohio corn, and for variation, a Michigan apple pie! (A real adventure in experimental dining for our midwestern friends, wouldn't you say??)

But no more! We've changed, the world has changed and so can you. We are all learning to be more health conscious, to eat lighter, lower fat meals. So remember, your guests no doubt share your attitudes and will appreciate lighter cuisine. (We've met very few tourists who take a Florida vacation to try to get their weight and cholesterol UP!)

SO READ OUR HIPS! NO HEAVY MEALS!

And what better place can there possibly be to cook fresh and light than Florida? With our twelve month growing and fishing seasons, local produce and seafood markets abound with tropical goodies year round. So take advantage of them - experiment.

Just going to the markets is fun - a visual and sensual adventure. Encourage guests to go with you, or better yet, to go FOR you. They'll enjoy the experience and appreciate your tropical temptations even more.

With your cooking and your guests dining pleasure in mind we have developed ten days of specific meal plans, which include menus and recipes starting on page 39. The meals are light, simple to prepare, and include ingredients which are readily available, nutritious and delicious. We think they will be of great help to fledgling and battle-weary accidental hostesses alike, since everything you need is right here in this one book. But first, here are some general suggestions you should try:

■ Visit our wonderful fresh seafood markets often and be adventurous - try something new. We have included lots of fish and seafood recipes you can follow, but here are some general rules of thumb:

- Firm fleshed fish such as swordfish, salmon, or tuna are excellent grilled or broiled. Try a light flavorful marinade like Teriyaki or Mojo Criollo or just some lemon butter and Everglades seasoning.

- Finer fleshed fish are more delicate and better poached, sauteed, baked, or fried. Go easy on the seasonings or sauces so the flavor of the fish isn't overpowered.

- Try blackening grouper, snapper, or redfish for variety. The recipe and the seasonings are readily available on the Islands.

- Shellfish tend to be higher in cholesterol than other varieties so try preparing them with minimal additional fat. See our recipe for curried shrimp on page 96.

- A hearty chowder is an easy dinner after a busy day. It's also an ideal way to use your house guests' catch of the day. If the catch is meager, chowders can be augmented with frozen or canned fish you have on hand. We have included an excellent recipe on page 132.

- Fried fish is still a favorite and need not be oily or heavy if you follow our recipe carefully and use **very** hot oil. Instead of the traditional tartar sauce, try making it with a mixture of ½ yogurt and ½ light mayonnaise. It's delicious and better for you. See recipe on page 44.

- Get your guests to try smoked fish. It's probably not available at home, and is a unique island taste treat.

Once again, remember what a treat fresh seafood is if you come from Dead Tree, Kansas, or Horn Barn, Illinois. Your guests' idea of a great seafood dinner at home is probably frozen fish sticks with a canned sardine chaser. Indulge them with Florida's finest. It's easy, nutritious and drop dead delicious.

■ Don't overlook the novelty of fresh citrus. You may have a back yard full of it and get hives at the thought of another grapefruit, but your guests don't. They'll love the unique flavor of key limes with their beverages and probably rarely, if ever, drink grapefruit or orange juice at home which hasn't done time in the freezer. One of the biggest hits we've ever made with guests is to keep a large bowl of mixed citrus fruit on the kitchen counter with a juicer next to it. Combining fruits, and squeezing their way to health excites guests on a level we would reserve for intergalactic travel.

■ While in the citrus market check out other fresh fruits. They are usually available in infinite variety and at reasonable prices. Whether for breakfast, lunch, snacks, garnishes or deserts, fruit seems particularly compatible with our hot humid Florida climate. We have included several recipes for fruit dishes, but get creative and try your own combinations. One of our favorites for breakfast or desert is chilled Kiwi, strawberries and pineapple layered in a clear glass bowl. It's refreshing to the eye as well as the pallet. Remember, your guests come from the land of prunes and canned fruit cocktail. Let them enjoy a fiber frenzy a la tropical.

■ Don't forget to use "Flower Power." No, that doesn't mean giving your guests a wilted posy and the peace sign at the airport. Do it '90's style. Use our abundance of tropical flowers in your cooking and food presentations. Edible flowers are certainly the rage in funky California fern bars, but we are not suggesting that you dish up a Gut Busting Gardenia Goulash or a Frangipani Fricassee. You really need to know your stuff to pull that off and avoid poisoning your guests.

What we ARE suggesting is that you step into your yard and pluck a few lovelies and use them to garnish your meals. (Just be sure to DE-ANT them first - instructions follow!) With the abundance and variety of flowers available, let your imagination go wild. Even the simplest dishes take on designer status when served a la posy. The Accidental Hostess assures you, once you get into Flower Power, you'll swear off parsley forever.

To de-ant a flower:

1. Immerse it carefully in very cold water for several minutes or until you notice little ant corpses floating to the surface.
2. Remove it from the water and drain gently on paper towels.
3. Check for survivors. If any linger, repeat steps 1 and 2.
4. Store de-anted flowers in zip-lock baggies in the refrigerator. This step is very important for it serves a two fold purpose. a) It keeps flowers dewy fresh until serving time and b) It puts any possible remaining plucky little SUPER ANTS in a comatose state. With any luck at all, they won't revive until the meal is completed.
(A word of caution: DO NOT SPRAY FLOWERS WITH RAID! It kills the flower as well as the ants and neither the flavor nor aroma tend to compliment food.)

Again, use flowers lavishly to garnish meals. It's easy, cheap and will knock the folks from Bleak Prairie, Minnesota off their pins. Remember, their idea of flowers in February is probably a dusty plastic rose in a dark green bud vase on top of the TV.

- Jump on the fresh veggie bandwagon. They are available and inexpensive year-around and come in mind-staggering varieties. Select them with reckless abandon. (One of us recently bought a little number looking mighty like a squash, only rounder - smelling like a cabbage only stronger - and tasting like a cucumber, only crunchier. It was delicious, but what was it? Maybe a squacabumber?)

We have included some yummy and easy veggie recipes in this book, but remember our cardinal rule when you try them:

THOU SHALT NOT OVERCOOK THY VEGETABLES!

Your guests will soon be back in Frozen Faucet, Wisconsin, land of canned peas and succotash. While they are here, let them experience the vibrant color and titillating crunch of perfectly prepared vegetables. Or better yet, make it even easier on yourself and serve them raw. Cold crunchy raw vegetables with a light yogurt dip is a perfect snack on a hot humid day. (Also, with practice you can learn to create one mean palm tree garnish with a raw carrot and half a green pepper.)

½ Green Pepper and Carrot.

- If some of your guests have children, be sure to consider their special needs when planning meals and snacks. Ask their parents about special likes and dislikes or allergies to avoid waste, and remember, kids will be hot and sweaty and therefore thirsty most of the time. Keeping lots of light snacks, yogurt, pudding, jello, applesauce, and juice in the refrigerator will keep them happy between meals. One of our favorite tricks is to keep individual cartons of juice in the freezer. Take them along to the beach. They will be thawed and easy to serve when the kids are ready for a drink.

As you plan meals, plan at least a few dinners where the kids can eat early and then watch a video. Their dinner bell tends to ring earlier than adults. Once they are done eating and settled into an enjoyable activity, your adult guests can relax and enjoy your simple, yet exquisitely prepared meal and rave over your dewy fresh, de-anted hibiscus garnish.

We are almost done with generalities here - finally - but here are a few more suggestions to help make you a happy, charming accidental hostess, not a twitchy, raving accidental schizophrenic!

- If your guests offer to take you out for a meal,

FOR GOODNESS SAKES - LET THEM!

- If it's high season you may decide to reject a restaurant invitation because of the crowds. (Do think this through before you say "no" - would you rather wait a bit in a restaurant, sipping a tall tropical temptation, or slave over a hot sink at home de-anting hibiscus and crafting a palm tree from a carrot and half a green pepper?) But if you can't stand the crowds yet would love an evening where you are not shackled to a hot microwave, try this idea. Suggest your guests take you to dinner at HOME. They can plan the meal, do the shopping, preparation and clean-up while you have a manicure, take a leisurely bubble bath, or read a smut novel. It's fun and easy for all, especially you.

- Don't ever overlook that resplendent 20th century tradition - CARRY-OUT FOOD. It's available in delicious abundance on the islands, and indeed in most resort areas, and can be a major sanity saver. Also, try to establish the tradition that on carry-out nights THEY carry it out, not you. (And if per chance the carry-out concessionaire expects to be **paid** at the time of out-carrying, well, that can work out nicely too.)

- Comb the yellow pages, the newspaper and road signs for those two little words which put new meaning in life and bring glee to the heart of every accidental hostess. "WE DELIVER". It doesn't matter what; who cares? If they want to deliver it, LET 'EM! Oh, and if your guests are the type who head for the restroom when the check comes in a restaurant, turn the tables and do the same when the door bell rings at home, reminding them that large tips for delivery are "customary" on the island.

Well, that pretty well wraps up generalities. Now for specifics. And our specifics are pretty specific. As noted earlier, we have painstakingly put together 10 days worth of menus, (3 meals per day,) that are easy to prepare, delicious, and healthy. We have included all recipes, tested exhaustingly by our exclusive panel of discriminating house guests. Simply pick a day, follow the recipes and instructions carefully, and voila, you are in business. . . . . It's a piece of cake, (low caloric and cholesterol of course).

So go for it, Hostesses. Do your own thing, or use the suggestions, recipes and meal plans you find here. We guarantee you'll produce meals which will dazzle your guests so simply that you'll still have time and energy left over to work on that palm tree made out of a carrot and a green pepper.

CATEGORY II

DEAR FRIENDS:

Actually, there are several varieties of DEAR FRIENDS. DEAR DEAR FRIENDS are like family, and should be treated as such (See Category I, page 5). But there's a vast spectrum of others, ranging from "QUITE DEAR" to "HOW-DE-DO, TOO-DA-LOO" which we will address in this section.

The Accidental Hostess's job, and it is a vitally important one, is to differentiate between them, plot them appropriately on the old "FRIEND-O-METER," (see below) and once plotted, to entertain them accordingly. (We'll help you with suggestions on how to entertain the range of friends from "QUITE DEAR" to "MARGINALLY GOOD." Those who fall below the "MARGINALLY GOOD" line should be downgraded to Category III).

FRIEND-O-METER

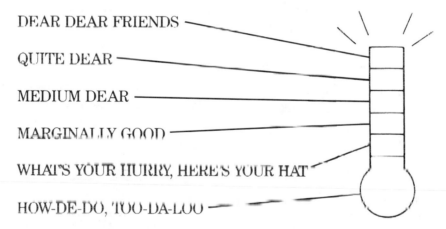

DEAR DEAR FRIENDS

QUITE DEAR

MEDIUM DEAR

MARGINALLY GOOD

WHAT'S YOUR HURRY, HERE'S YOUR HAT

HOW-DE-DO, TOO-DA-LOO

But this is no easy task, for you'll have many contenders for this coveted classification. Since most of us are kind of heart and generous of spirit, we tend to plot far too many folks on the "QUITE DEAR" end of our FRIEND-O-METER and this is a major mistake. If we're not careful, we can end up with more "QUITE DEAR" friends than Tammy Faye Bakker has make-up tips. And unlike Tammy's credo, when it comes to "QUITE DEAR" friends, **MORE is NOT BETTER!**

So think carefully about who your "QUITE DEAR" to "MARGINALLY GOOD" friends are. We really can't be of much help at this task, but here are some tips on who these friends are **NOT!**

- Your ex-sister-in-law, the whining nail-biter with the tick, whose contribution to **ALL** those holiday dinners at **YOUR** house was the salt and pepper...she, and her fifth husband, and two year old are **NOT** medium dear friends!

- Your son's old calculus teacher, the bespectacled egg-head with the lisp, who now grows rhubarb in Dead Possum, Tennessee, but who still loves a lively evening conversation about the square root of 2 to the 10th power, is **NOT** a medium dear friend.

- Your husband's old boss, the wheezing back-slapper with dandruff, who never travels without his 200 pound drooling bull mastiff, Spike, is definitely **NOT** a medium dear friend.

- Your old dentist's **NEW** hygienist, the frizzy headed mini-skirted size 18 with the two children who whine and the two who bite, and who wrote the booklet - **The Root Canal: Your Waterway to Oral Ecstasy** is **NOT** a medium dear friend.

- Your old dentist's **OLD** hygienist, the near sighted plaque buster with halitosis, who thinks a root canal is a tributary of the Amazon River which is just south of Cleveland, is definitely **NOT** a medium dear friend either.

With practice, you'll learn to spot these folks easily, plot them on the low end of the FRIEND-O-METER, down grade them to a Category III and dismiss them quickly. Remember, if they wouldn't be calling you if you lived in Dead Tree, Oklahoma, you don't have to wine them and dine them on Sanibel. A polite "HOW-DE-DO" and a quick "TOO-DA-LOO" will do!

To help you develop a harder shell and a tougher attitude, consider this scenario:

The phone rings; you answer:

"Hello?"

"Hey ...,"

"Hey?"

"I bet you don't know who this is!"

"Well ... no."

"Take a guess, Yuk, Yuk!"

"I really have no idea . . ."

"Come on! One guess. Yuk, Yuk"

"DONALD TRUMP?"

"Guess again, you ole kidder you! Yuk, Yuk, Yuk."

"JIMMY SWAGGART?"

"Still have the ole sense of humor, eh? Yuk, Yuk."

"Who is this?"

"It's Ralph . . . Ralph Nerdley - from Parched Prairie."

"Oh . . . Ralph? Hey?"

"HEY!"

"Sooooooo, Ralph."

"Sooo!. We're in the area and we'd **love** to see you!"

"Hey, that's . . . that's great, Ralph. Gee, we'd love to see you too."

"HEY!"

"Hey? How about, ummmm . . . Saturday. We could go out in the boat, er . . . do some fishing, maybe come back here for a picnic?"

"HEY! That'd be **great!** The kids **love** to fish!"

"KIDS?"

"Yeah, Ralphy's twelve now, Sissy's eleven, Brucy's ten and little Matthew's two. We call him Matt the Brat! Yuk, Yuk, Yuk."

"Well, that's quite a family, Ralph. Say . . . well, we'll look forward to Saturday then!"

So what's wrong with this conversation? Well, basically EVERYTHING! You've been caught off guard and you've lost control of the situation. Ralph and his family should be on the "HOW-DE DO" and "TOO-DA-LOO" end of the FRIEND-O-METER, but instead, you'll be entertaining all of them all weekend. And worst of all,

YOU BROUGHT IT ON YOURSELF!

Let's try it again picking up at those five little words we warned you to beware of . . .

"We'd love to see you."

"That'd be fun Ralph - where are you staying?"

"Well we aren't sure yet, but . . ."

"Well give me a call back when you're settled and we'll work something out. Nice talking to you, How-De-Doo."

There, that's better . . . Now YOU'RE IN CONTROL - you have options. You can see Ralph, and Sissy and Brucy and whoever when, where and for as long as **YOU** want to.

By the time he calls back, they'll have a place to stay and you'll have a plan for seeing them which is consistent with both your schedule and Ralph's lowly position on the FRIEND-O-METER.

So once again, remember, the time you spend with friends, be they "MEDIUM DEAR," "MARGINALLY GOOD," "HOW-DE-DOO-TOO-DA-LOO" or anything in between, should be controlled by **YOU** and fit into **YOUR** schedule. If you let your guests, even very special ones, take over your calendar and control your life, you'll end up a blubbering frustrated ying-yang instead of a charming, albeit accidental hostess.

But let's look for a minute at really great, special friends, those above the Marginally Good Line. You don't want them living with you (they probably don't either) but you'd really love to see them and show them a lovely time. The trick here is to plan a specific activity at a specific time. Be sure your guests know exactly:

- What activity is planned.
- During what hours.
- What dress is appropriate.
- What to bring (i.e. towels, dramamine, a good waterproof mascara . . .).

NEVER issue a nebulous, open ended invitation like "Drop by anytime - we're always around."

When it comes to the planning of an activity, use your imagination, letting interests and ages be your guide. There are lots of suggestions in the Category I section of this book (page 5) and you'll no doubt add many of your own. But to start you off, here are some sure-fun-for-everyone activities you might like to plan. We've included menus and recipes to make your job as designated food wench a lot easier. (See page 101.)

- *Have a picnic at the beach.* Now you can't miss with this one. With the sun dancing on the Gulf of Mexico, the pelicans performing their synchronized aerial maneuvers and the sugar white sand, bejeweled with shells, you have a picture perfect setting for a day in paradise. Just pick your favorite beach, arm yourselves with sunscreen, shell bags and beach toys, and have at one of Sanibel's favorite pastimes. And be sure to take along all the goodies from our "PICNIC ON THE BEACH" menu (page 102). They're easy to prepare and pack, and will hit the spot after a refreshing swim, or a grueling sand castle contest.

- *Spend the day boating with lunch aboard.* Take your pick of the vast variety of boating experiences available in this water wonderland. Try some offshore fishing or sailing in the majestic Gulf; do a little gunkholing in the mangrove-tangled islands of the back bays; or take a slow, leisurely cruise up our own Old Man River, the Caloosahatchee. If you're fortunate enough to own a boat, you're all set. If not, there are many charters available around the islands both bare boat and captained. Check the weather and the tides, grab your chart and pack the cooler with our "DAY ON THE WATER" lunch (page 105).

- *Try a Workout Cookout Party.* The workout can be any sport you all enjoy - tennis, golf, biking, fishing or a pep-step hike on the beach. A cool down cookout in your yard is a perfect way for your guests to wind down into a noncompetitive mode. Try our WORKOUT - COOKOUT menu (page 108) and your guests will think you've won the Coveted-Captiva-Cook-Till-You Croak contest!

- *Share a legendary Sanibel Sunset with your guests, followed by a dinner al fresco, under the stars.* You probably have a favorite sunset spot, but if not, the causeway Islands are a lovely place to view nature's daily grand finale. As the sunset colors subside, the talismans of tropical evenings arrive as dinner guests: Orion, Taurus, and of course the Dipper Duo, Big and Little putting magic into the evening and more than compensating for the pesky no-seeums. Dish up our DROP-DEAD-GREAT-DINNER-FOR-EIGHT (page 112) while you enjoy Sanibel at its loveliest with your friends. And by the way, if your yard is not appointed with the understated elegance of Ralph Lauren's latest "Instant Tradition" collection of patio furniture, card tables and candles work very nicely.

- *Plan a Night at the Theater, followed by dessert and coffee back at your home.* Excellent local theater groups abound on the islands, both professional and amateur. The quality of the performance plus the ambience of our intimate, albeit makeshift theaters will contribute to an evening your guests will long remember. For your own rendition of a curtain call, serve our AFTER THEATER DESSERT AND COFFEE menu (page 116). The Pot-Au-Chocolate is great, and as an encore, hit 'em with one of our Special Coffees. They're each TO DIE FOR!

■ *Plan an old friends meet new friends cocktail party.* One of the most frustrating aspects of constant out of town guests is the fact that while you are busy seeing old friends, you neglect seeing your new local friends. By having a cocktail party including both old and new, you can, as they say, "kill two birds with one stone." (The Accidental Hostess knows what they mean by this dumb metaphor, but isn't sure why anyone would want to kill any birds!) If you don't want to serve mixed drinks, try just beer and wine, or make a blender full of our easy frozen daiquiris (page 128). Slam out a few of our simple yet yummy hors d'oeuvres from our OLD FRIENDS MEET NEW FRIENDS menu (page 120), dish them up with abundant amounts of island ambience, and voilà, you've got yourself a night of no fuss fun.

If you've ever taken scuba lessons, you no doubt remember the cardinal rule:

"PLAN YOUR DIVE and DIVE YOUR PLAN!"

If you don't, you'll run out of **AIR!**

The Accidental Hostess believes the same principle applies to entertaining out of town guests.

"PLAN YOUR ENTERTAINING AND ENTERTAIN YOUR PLAN!"

If you don't you'll run out of **GAS!**

So here's our final overall scoop. Plan fun, interesting, island oriented activities with your visiting friends. Serve them food which is elegant, easy, and a bit different than what they're used to at home. Do your entertaining ISLAND STYLE taking advantage of the vast and varied resources available here. And last, but definitely most importantly - STAY IN CONTROL OF THE SITUATION. Be in charge of how, when and where you entertain your friends.

DROP-INS

"Drop-Ins" is an acronym. It stands for **D**on't **R**eally **O**ffend **P**eople, but **I**nterrupt their **N**ormal **S**cene. (Sometimes we feel more like it stands for **D**umb, **R**otten, **O**bnoxious **P**ests who **I**ntrude, are a **N**uisance and are **S**tupid!) Drop-Ins are people who we know slightly, or not at all, who are "in town" and who just show up on our doorsteps. They don't write, call or announce their impending arrival in any way. They just arrive.

Drop-Ins are also a very diverse group - and a huge one. We've heard of DROP-INS ranging from the guy who used to date the girlfriend of the drummer who used to play at our favorite night spot in Lake Toxic Waste, N.C., to the brother of our old veterinarian's assistant, who our dog bit while getting a flea dip, from Big Cloud, Montana. We've heard of DROP-INS whose only link to us is that our children met thirteen years ago while starring together in a cat food commercial- the one whose kid dropped out because he was allergic to cats.

DROP-INS are a very diverse group indeed, but we've also noticed a thread of peculiar and unbecoming similarities which bind them together into a cohesive group. For instance, we've noticed that a disproportionate number of DROP-INS have recently **DROPPED OUT,** and are embarking upon a Quixotic search for their elusive true selves, starting on our door steps. Also, we've found that a whopping 87% of our sample group of DROP-INS have **DROPPED THE BALL** in the old make Room Reservations department, and pick up quickly on carelessly dropped phrases like "Guest Room!" And we also suspect, although conclusive evidence is unavailable, that to most DROP-INS, we could **DROP DEAD** for all they care, except for the fact that we live in the land of sun and fun - Vacationville U.S.A.

Of course, there are some GOOD DROP-INS - nice folks who really want to see us and have no hidden agenda. They just don't happen to have the foresight to use the telephone or the Postal Service.

But, together with the BAD DROP-INS, they share this single unfortunate characteristic, which lumps them together in this lowly Category III.

THEY DON'T ANNOUNCE THEIR IMPENDING ARRIVAL.
THEY JUST SHOW UP!

They are frequently hungry, occasionally thirsty, usually roomless, and **ALWAYS UNEXPECTED.**

Now this doesn't necessarily mean we don't want to see them or aren't glad they stopped. It's just that they're unexpected, it's inconvenient and we're unprepared.

So what do we do? How do we cope? Let's try our hypothetical scenario again, this time starting with the door bell:

"Yes, can I help you?"

"Mary? Mary Boyes! Why, you haven't changed a bit! I'd know you anywhere! How the **heck** are you?"

"Ummmm . . . fine? How are you?"

"You don't remember me, do you?"

"Well, you look familiar? Well . . . actually, no. No, I don't!"

"It's Zeek . . . Zeek Kowolski! From Tippy Canoe High School, in Wisconsin!"

"Zeek? Zeek the Geek? I can't believe it!"

"Yip, it's me! Well, how ya been?"

"Well . . . fine Zeek. Just fine. How have you been?"

"Oh! GREAT! JUST GREAT!"

"Well,er . . . won't you, um . . . won't you come in?"

Now let's stop right here - you've made your first mistake. Ole Zeek the Geek might have been a dynamite chemistry lab partner in Tippy Canoe High School in 1958, but for all you know, he's spent the last 30 years as an axe murderer, or more likely as a professional freeloader. So here's our RULE # 1 REGARDING DROP-INS.

IF YOU DON'T KNOW THEM, OR BARELY KNOW THEM, YOU ARE NOT OBLIGATED TO INVITE THEM IN. IN FACT WISDOM DICTATES THAT YOU DON'T.

With practice, you'll learn to politely but firmly explain that they've caught you at a busy time, but if they'll be in town for a while, they're welcome to call you later to make plans to get together. This is not rude or inhospitable - it is **smart** and **necessary.** It's absolutely essential that you take charge of the situation and stay in control. The consequences of doing otherwise are pretty scary!

But let's get back to ole Zeek, who is now standing in your living room, and seems to be making himself right at home. It's too late to avoid the situation. So let's try to get out of it.

The key is to set a time limit on the visit immediately, and be sure Zeek knows what it is. Don't get sucked into a protracted "so what have you been up to for the last 30 years?" type conversation. That can come later, **if you so desire, at your convenience.** Try this approach:

"So Mary, what have you been up to these last 30 years!"

"Gee Zeek, we have a lot of catching up to do, don't we? But I'm afraid it can't be today. I have appointments starting in about ten minutes and going into the evening. Why don't you give me a call tomorrow, if you'll still be in the area, and we can work out a time to visit."

At this point, if you care to, you can offer Zeek a cold drink or a comfortable seat, but you've established the fact that this will be a short visit, and in ten minutes, you'll be out of there and **SO WILL HE.** Now, you have time to decide if and when you want a longer visit with ole Zeek, and make plans accordingly.

Of course, not all Drop-Ins are as unwelcome or as inconvenient as Zeek. Occasionally, you'll no doubt find yourself sitting idly on a lovely March afternoon. You're immaculately groomed, perfectly coiffed and have just arranged a lovely bouquet of fresh flowers, (a gift from recent houseguests) in a lovely crystal vase, (a gift from other recent houseguests) for your just dusted coffee table in your recently redecorated living room - from your kitchen, the aroma of bread baking, from the garden the aroma of flowers blooming. The setting is sublime, but alas there's no one there to share it. Your mind drifts off to your recent around-the-world cruise and the delightfully witty yet charmingly eccentric couple you met, and with whom you shared so many evenings of stimulating conversation about diverse yet shared interests. Your reverie is interrupted by a sudden DING DONG and, as you answer the door, you are delighted beyond description to see the very objects of your wistful daydream standing on your front porch. "OOOHHH - HOW DO, HOW DO, COME IN, COME IN."

Remember we said you'd "occasionally" experience this kind of Drop-In encounter. Well occasionally is a pretty nebulous word, so to help you pin down the likelihood of this happening, let us say we've lived here for a cumulative total of twenty-four years and are still waiting . . . The "If I knew you were coming I'd a Baked a Cake", kind of Drop-Ins are theoretically possible. But our experience says the "If I knew you were coming, I'd a moved away!" type are a heck of a lot more common.

And of course there are a lot of cases in between the "I'd a baked a cake" and the "I'd a moved away" types. Some drop-ins are a delightful surprise, even if the timing is not ideal. Sometimes the timing is ideal even if the Drop-Ins are not a delightful surprise. And in between there are lots and lots of variables and situations. But the rule to handling any and all Drop-Ins, regardless of the degree of enthusiasm with which you greet them is the same and it is this:

YOU TAKE CONTROL OF THE SITUATION AND STAY IN CHARGE!

If you're delighted to see them and want to invite them for a longer visit - fine - do it, but at your convenience. If you don't want to see them - DON'T. It's just that simple. You are under no obligation, moral, social, legal or otherwise to entertain uninvited, unexpected guests. Do what **YOU WANT,** not what you think **THEY WANT,** or what you think is expected, and you'll do just fine.

Throughout the **ACCIDENTAL HOSTESS** you'll find recipes useful for Drop-Ins who you **WANT** to see and who arrive at **CONVENIENT** times. They're easy, quick and made with ingredients you'll usually have on hand. But again, don't feel obligated - do and serve only what you want.

Also, in case you lose it momentarily, throw all our advice to the wind, and wind up with a table full of unexpected Drop-Ins at meal time, use our **DESPERATION DINNER** menu (page 27). It's a lot of work, but well worth the effort for the results surely justify the time and expense. We unconditionally guarantee your Drop-Ins will NEVER return, and our most recent polls show over 73% leave before the second course is served.

DESPERATION DINNER MENU

- Oysters on the Whole Shell
- Marcella's Liver and Red Onions
- Twice Boiled Swiss Chard
- Half-baked Potatoes with Imitation Bacon Bits
- Wonderbread with Uncolored Margarine
- Milk Shake (Fast Food Variety)

OYSTERS ON THE WHOLE SHELL (Serves 6)

INGREDIENTS: 6 oysters in their shell

PREPARATION: Place whole, unopened oysters on a platter garnished with parsley and fresh flowers. Serve in the living room with cocktails. (We recommend a nice flat, warm Club Soda with an olive to accompany this dish. Be sure to provide cocktail napkins and small hors d'oeuvres plates for each guest. Be sure to omit any type of oyster knife or sauce. This way guests will be unable to open the oysters and you can return them to the ice and enjoy them yourselves later.

MARCELLA'S LIVER WITH RED ONIONS (Serves 6)

INGREDIENTS: 1 lb. old cow liver
(bull liver preferable if available)
½ red onion - sliced
2 T lard

PREPARATION: Buy liver ahead and allow to ripen in the hot sun for 3 days. Freeze until needed. Melt lard in black skillet over high heat 'till it starts to smoke. Add liver and cook one hour over high heat, or until it is the consistency of a Goodyear Radial Snow Tire. Add red onions and cook till they start to turn a greenish color. Serve at once with twice boiled Swiss chard. (This doesn't make much, but it goes a long way).

TWICE BOILED SWISS CHARD

(Serves 6)

INGREDIENTS: 2 lbs. Swiss chard
                      3 qts. water
                      3 qts. water

PREPARATION: Select the oldest, toughest Swiss chard available. Remove any tender lighter green leafy sections and discard. Do not wash as this removes the flavorful morsels of sand and grit. Bring first 3 qts. of water to a boil. Boil, covered one hour. Drain. (This first boiling removes all vitamins and nutrients). Bring second 3 qts. of water to a boil and return Swiss chard to pot. Boil one additional hour or until any remaining color in the leaves is removed. Drain and serve at once. (It should be the consistency of limp celery strings).

CHOCOLATE MILK SHAKES

(Serves 6)

INGREDIENTS: 6 fast food chocolate milk shakes
                      6 serving glasses
                      6 maraschino cherries

PREPARATION: Buy milk shakes early in the day and set out on counter. At serving time, transfer into serving glasses and garnish with cherry. Serve at your leisure. You'll be delighted how these milk shakes retain their original texture and consistency despite the fact that they've been at room temperature all day.

# CATEGORY IV

SPRING BREAKERS

Theoretically it is possible to live in Florida and not know what Spring Breakers are, (though realistically you'd have to be deaf, dumb, blind and comatose to miss them). But for the sake of clarity and to maintain the consistently high standards for preciseness established in this work, we'll define them.

Spring Breakers are normally serious college students on a one week furlough from northern universities. They make a major road trip (24 hours straight at a minimum) to Florida's beaches each spring in search of a brief respite from sleet, slush, snow and studies, a serious tan (one which causes blisters and peeling of the top seven layers of skin) and a rocking hot time.

They are most easily recognized by their dress, or shall we say uniforms:

■ Long baggy shorts, preferably torn, with anything from a minor hint to a major display of underwear peeking through from beneath.

■ A huge T-shirt (size XXL minimum) preferably with an important message ("DON'T WORRY, BE ANGRY") and always a bit torn.

■ An optional huge tank top (size XXXL minimum) over the T-shirt. (If the T-shirt's message is poignant enough to stand alone, the tank is unnecessary.)

■ A pair of $150.00 high top basketball shoes, unlaced of course. Air Jordans are the brand of choice, but others are acceptable if they have the obligatory adjustable air space between the layers to compensate for the high impact nature of the sport for which they are intended - sort of an inflatable version of our generation's P.F. Flyers! These shoes are optional if you happen to actually play basketball, but essential if you do not!

■ A pair of $250.00 designer sun glasses (the brand depends on the college from which the Spring Breakers matriculate, but Ray Bans, Varnet and Sun Cloud are usually good).

Beneath this "dress wear" is worn the beach wear. For boys the baggiest of swim trunks are in order. For girls the briefest of bikinis, the price of which is inversely proportional to the amount of fabric used in their construction.

All in all, Spring Breakers seem to try to achieve a look which says "I've been living in a car or sleeping on a beach for a week!" This look, of course, is not difficult to achieve, as most of them **have been.** (Of course a few of the fussier types rent a class C motel room which they share, until evicted, with 12 - 18 of their closest friends.)

The second easy way to identify Spring Breakers is by their language. They've developed their own, a kind of **BREAK-SPEAK,** and although it is similar to English, it's pure simplicity of structure makes it unlike any other form of communication known to civilized man. You see, BREAK-SPEAK has no nouns or verbs or other common parts of speech. It's a language of SUPERLATIVES only: "BAD," "SWEET," "COUGE," "SCARY," "GIIIIT," and our personal favorite "DOUJZED"! (We're not exactly sure what "Doujzed" means, but we're pretty sure the connotation does not involve taking your clothes off!) Each of these words, despite the frequency of their use, is uttered with an inflection which implies that a truth of global or cosmic importance has just been uttered. And for even more emphasis, for comments of significance barely imaginable to the mere mortal man, the impact of any of these superlatives can be doubled, even squared, by adding the prefix **"TOTALLY!"** Can you even comprehend the **AMAZINGNESS of being "TOTALLY DOUJZED?"**

If dress and language fail to tip you off as to who the Spring Breakers are, we recommend looking for these traits as well:

- They tend to both hang out and travel in packs of twelve to twenty.

- Their music comes in decibel levels to which jack hammer operators twitch and stray dogs howl.

- Their cars (and we use the term loosely) are of a vintage possibly viewed as desirable by the proprietors of the Rothchild wine cellars, but definitely not by the editors of Motor Trend magazine.

- Despite the fact that many of them are our future dieticians and nutritionists, they live on a diet of twinkies, nachos, popcorn and beer.

- They are nocturnal. They may crawl out of bed by the crack of noon, but then it's right back to sleep on the beach. They don't begin to wake up 'till the sun begins to go down.

■ Also despite the fact that they are the beneficiaries of $60,000.00 educations, they are penniless - "TOTALLY"! They can somehow produce the funds for necessities (like **BEER**), but luxuries (**FOOD** and **HOUSING**) are out, and must be picked up catch as catch can wherever available.

This last characteristic, that of being TOTALLY PENNILESS is the reason Spring Breakers are included in **THE ACCIDENTAL HOSTESS,** for there is nothing so cherished on a northern college campus as a friend from Florida - especially a friend from Sanibel or Captiva Island. Such a prized friendship translates in literal terms to **"FREE ROOM AND BOARD FOR SPRING BREAK!"** Those of you who are parents of college age students already know all about this. Those of you who have small children have these experiences to look forward to. And even those of you with grown children aren't immune, for grandchildren eventually attend college too. And we promise you, your turn will come to receive that classic phone call:

Ri-nn-ng!

"Hello"

"Will you accept the charges?"

"Hi Mom!"

"Hi Honey, what's the matter . . . you sound sick."

"I am, Mom, it's soooo cold here! I can't stand it."

"Well, spring break is not too far away and you can come home and enjoy the Florida sun."

"I know, I can't wait! Cough, cough, cough, **COUGH, COUGH, COUGH, COUGH!"**

"My God, who's that?"

"It's Cynthia. She's cold and sick too! Do you think maybe she can come home with me for spring break?"

"Of course, your friends are always welcome."

"Actually, a few other friends are really cold and sick. Is it okay if they come along?"

"Well, I guess so. Just keep it down to a reasonable number."

Let's stop right here. "A reasonable number!" Let's think about that one. In The Accidental Hostess's opinion, agreeing with your child on what a reasonable number is, is about as likely as agreeing with her on the choice of a radio station in the car. (On the writer's first encounter with Spring Breakers, her daughter picked the reasonable number of **SIXTEEN** to spend the week!)

So here's our first bit of advice, and it will sound familiar: **YOU** stay in control and **YOU** decide how many people you can and are willing to have as houseguests for a week.

And we also recommend that you make a very conservative decision on numbers of guests, for we guarantee it will be ouched up quite a bit by the time they arrive.

And here's our next bit of wisdom. Get a list of names, first and LAST, and their parents' phone numbers, and be sure the kids know that only invited and expected guests will be accommodated. Let them know BEFORE their arrival that they will be guests in your home and accountable to you, not interchangeable bodies doing DOWN time at the No-Tell-Motel. To keep even a shred of sanity, you'll need to know who is staying with you and who isn't, and they'll need to know that you know.

Okay, so we've established that you'll decide how many Spring Breakers you'll have, and you'll know who they are and they'll know who you are. So let's get to the nitty gritty of how you deal with them - the dope on how to cope.

But before we get into that, just a note to our diverse group of readers. These suggestions don't just apply to entertaining college kids. They should be helpful for entertaining any large group of houseguests, or even just meal guests - class reunions, special occasions, family reunions, etc. Also they should be very helpful to those of you who live in small condominiums with limited facilities or have interval weeks on the Islands and find your two week vacation becomes an exercise in entertaining casts of thousands.

In the family section of this manual we divided the how to cope suggestions into three parts: Accommodations, Activities and Meals. For continuity's sake we'll do that again in this section but you'll notice the suggestions are much different. For your family houseguests, we urged you to take the extra time to make things as comfy, and pretty and yummy as possible. We DO NOT recommend that in this section. The reason is simple . . . . . IT IS IMPOSSIBLE! For large groups of houseguests, be they children, teens, adults or any combination thereof, you must simply do the best you can with what you've got, and let it go at that. If your guests prefer a more gracious style of vacation, there are plenty of motels around.

Here then are our suggestions. We hope they'll help, but remember through it all - entertaining large groups isn't easy and if things don't seem to go as smoothly as you'd hoped, forget it. We're proud of you to even try!

ACCOMMODATIONS:

If you happen to have ten to fifteen empty bedrooms in your home or condo, you're in luck! If, like most of us, you DON'T, read on and take heart. The ole "many more bodies than beds" dilemma is not an easy nut to crack, but you'll just have to power through it. Try these approaches:

■ THE EVERY MAN FOR HIMSELF APPROACH:

Make a pile of all the sheets, blankets, pillows, towels sleeping bags and quilts you own and simply let them have at 'em. ("The first man to the bed gets it" sort of thing.) This works well with children and college kids as long as you have designated SLEEPING areas and designated NON-SLEEPING areas. (i.e. the bath tub is okay - under the coffee table is not!)

■ THE MUSICAL BED APPROACH:

Typically the last group in at night is the last up in the morning, and this can present a problem as they most likely get the least desirable sleeping area (under the dining room table, or the kitchen floor). This is fine for them, but makes morning coffee hour unpleasant for the MASTER BEDROOM dwellers. The "early to bed, early to rise" set feel neither healthy, wealthy nor wise when they have to enjoy their paper and coffee in the same room with four semi-comatose bodies. So here's the trick. As soon as a bedroom is vacated, herd the late sleepers from the living room into it - blankets, bed-heads and all. This is an effective, albeit less than totally gracious way to maximize minimal space.

■ THE STUFF STOPS HERE APPROACH:

Sometimes space is so limited, or bodies so numerous you simply can't have designated sleeping areas. In this case, to maintain at least some degree of order, have an area, or room set up to hold gear - bedding, clothing, towels, etc. Ask guests to keep all their stuff in this area, and if any is left lying around, you put it there. Granted, this room will be a total PIT, but at least the rest of the living area won't be.

Again, these aren't ideal solutions, but maybe they'll help a little. Remember, our overall message here is:

WHEN THE GOING GETS ROUGH - LOWER YOUR STANDARDS!

With perseverance, a sense of humor and a few trips to your favorite neighborhood shrink, you'll get through it.

ACTIVITIES:

Under the family section, we listed jillions of activities to entertain your guests. But for large groups:

FORGET IT!

It's impossible to organize large groups, be they college kids or not, to participate in a single activity. Our advice is - LET THEM ENTERTAIN THEMSELVES! There's plenty to do if they choose to, but most large groups, especially kids, like to just hang out in the sun and work on their tan. If you try to organize major outings, say to the bird sanctuary or the lighthouse, you'll make yourself crazy and your guests too. So we suggest you avoid a long losing battle by giving up early! Just let them do what they want, they know what that is, and if you simply **must** plan some organized fun, make it for yourself!

MEALS:

Here's where we get to the nitty gritty of entertaining Spring Breakers or any other cast of thousands. As we said earlier, not all members of your group will do their power sleeping at your home, but without exception,

THEY NEVER MISS A MEAL!

They also seem to have insatiable appetites and an ability to stock pile calories that leads one to believe if the great famine ever comes, Spring Breakers will be the last survivors on earth. So when planning meals for this extremely hungry and relatively indiscriminating crowd, remember:

QUANTITY COUNTS - QUALITY DOESN'T!

Now we're not suggesting you feed them Alpo with Bosco Sauce because they'll never know the difference. We're just saying,

GO FOR THE VOLUME AND VALUE APPROACH - NOT THE NOVELLE CUISINE, LESS IS MORE APPROACH.

Spring Breakers in particular, and other large groups of houseguests in general, do not measure your cuisine by a very sophisticated yard-stick. Perfectly prepared fish and vegetables are lost on them. Their idea of a great meal is one that makes them **SWEAT!** Their typical expression of appreciation for a particularly fine feed is **"GREAT GRUNTS, MOM!"**

So again, go for the greatest output of calories per dollar and energy expenditure. Don't forget quality totally, but it shouldn't be a hang-up. Remember where they're coming from - DORM FOOD! If they expect designer cuisine at a freeloader price, they're out of luck.

But again, the Accidental Hostess's cockeyed optimism says it's not impossible to combine ease of preparation with modest expenditure and relatively high palate pleasure. As before, we offer both general suggestions and specific recipes to help you through any and all major mobs.

Let's start with GENERAL SUGGESTIONS:

■ Serve all meals buffet style and if possible, outdoors. (If it's raining, bring an umbrella!)

■ Get into the disposable mode. Use every disposable time saver you can find, from Aluminum foil to Zip-lock baggies. Go for paper plates, bowls, cups, napkins, even pots and pans if you can find them.

■ The disposable advice ends with flatware - sort of. Do buy plastic utensils, but DO NOT pitch them. They go through the dishwasher well, and can be reused.

■ Take advantage of SLAVE LABOR. Pick 2 or 3 grunts per meal and sock it to 'em. They won't mind, really, and you'll be eternally grateful for their help. (Among their jobs can be to wash, sort and zip-lock baggie the plastic utensils.)

■ Plan menus by selecting items from the four major food groups college kids are accustomed to: **SALTS, SUGARS, ADDITIVES** and **PRESERVATIVES!**

- Never serve more food than you think they'll eat with "leftovers" in mind. There will be NO LEFTOVERS. They EAT EVERYTHING - always.

- Try cooking a turkey for lunch. Really, it's cheap, yummy and a roaring success. Don't mess with any frills - just roast the sucker and set it out with sandwich stuff. But don't count on any leftovers, (see above).

- Don't overlook old favorites. Spaghetti, hot dogs and burgers are always a hit.

- Tacos are a great crowd pleaser. Just set out the ingredients and let them make their own.

- Pasta salads always sell well. Don't worry about a recipe. Use any kind of noodle, any kind of vegetable and a healthy hit of mayonnaise. They'll love it.

- Kids really like to make their own breakfast, so for goodness sake, LET THEM. Just set out breads, cereals, juice, whatever and they'll fix their own as they stagger in.

- Be sure everyone knows when meals will be served, and that if they want to eat, they'd better be there. You DO NOT want to be dishing up one continuous feed from dawn to dusk.

As far as particulars for meals, we offer you a number of tried and true crowd pleasers, see page 129. They may not be the most unique or gourmet offerings you've ever found at the other end of a fork, but they're easy to prepare, inexpensive, filling and tasty. Give them a try the next time your gang shows up. We think you'll all be happy with the results.

Well, that about wraps up our words of wisdom for coping with constant company; but before we set you lose on your own we think it's worthwhile to recap and summarize our advice and suggestions.

First of all, you must realize that to live in a resort area is to entertain out of town guests - CONSTANTLY. So don't try to fight it, just work to manage it. The first step to managing it is to learn to prioritize your guests into these recommended categories: FAMILY, DEAR FRIENDS, DROP-INS and SPRING BREAKERS. We've listed these categories in descending order of desirability, and your expenditures of time, energy and money on any particular guest should be consistent with their position on this imaginary GUEST-O-GRAPH.

FAMILY members are on the top of the GUEST-O-GRAPH and therefore are top priority. But be careful who you consider to be "FAMILY." Theoretically we are all part of the family of man, and therefore related. But you must be much more selective in choosing family members to entertain as houseguests. Close or immediate family members should get and will appreciate your best efforts. Distant cousins or generic relative types need not and will not. Learn to be selective.

DEAR FRIENDS also come in a wide variety of sizes, shapes and degrees of desirability. They range from very special people you are delighted to see and entertain, to those who get in touch only when they're in town and need a place to stay. You must learn to differentiate between friends and entertain only those you really want to see. Use our suggested activities and menus and the job will be easy. But remember, DEAR FRIENDS is a category whose exclusive membership must be selected by you. It is not one into which any past acquaintance who happens to be in town can self-appoint himself.

DROP-INS are not necessarily undesirable guests, but they are frequently inconvenient and always unexpected. The challenge with these folks is to keep in total control of the situation; rather than entertain them when they show up, arrange a future mutually convenient time for a visit. And for those you don't wish to see later, you must learn to politely yet FIRMLY dismiss them with a "How-de-do, too-da-loo." And above all else, you must learn not to feel guilty about doing this; it's not rude or inhospitable - it's smart and necessary.

SPRING BREAKERS and other large crowds are the toughest nut to crack for their sheer numbers make them the hardest type of guests to keep under control.

Therefore our advice to you is just do the best you can with what you've got and let it go at that. Necessity dictates that accommodations and meals be kept as simple as possible, and organized group activities be avoided altogether. We recommend you avoid a long loosing battle to provide an atmosphere of gracious living by giving up early. And do remember our sage words of wisdom:

WHEN THE GOING GETS TOUGH, LOWER YOUR STANDARDS!

Don't be too hard on yourselves if you find your home more closely resembles a **FLOP-HOUSE-SOUP-KITCHEN** than a five star hotel. We're proud of you to even try this type of entertaining.

As for feeding the seemingly insatiable appetites of out of town guests, we've offered you many general suggestions, and even more specific menus and recipes. Read through them carefully, remember that they've all been exhaustingly tested by our discriminating panel of husbands and houseguests, and then pick and choose the ones which appeal to you or apply to your situation. Once you've done this, we feel confident sending you out there to the front lines of hostesshood, knowing you're ready to handle the challenge of this command: **"LADIES, START YOUR OVENS!"**

And finally, our message to you is to relax and have fun with this wild and wacky world of the accidental hostess. Lighten up, go with the flow, get a real life! **The School of Hard Knock, Knock, Knocks** isn't easy, but you're up to it and have great teachers. Besides, all tables eventually turn, and we unconditionally guarantee that your turn will come to be the INTENTIONAL TOURIST!

 # 10 DAYS AT A GLANCE

DAY ONE	DAY SIX
page 40 to 46	**page 71 to 75**
B - Orange French Toast	B - Orange Cream Cheese Spread
L - Sauteed Chicken Salad	L - Caesar Salad with French Bread
Pita Parmesan	D - Grilled Butterflied Leg of Lamb a la Betty
Nannie's Chocolate Chip Cookies	Boiled New Potatoes
D - Florida Fried Fish	Cauliflower Scramble
Stuffed Sweet Potato	Romaine and Mandarin Orange Salad
Steamed Broccoli	Grapes in a Goblet
Hearts of Palm Salad	
Hot Raspberry Sundae	

DAY TWO	DAY SEVEN
page 47 to 53	**page 76 to 81**
B - Barb's Breakfast Casserole	B - Apple Pancakes with Syrup
L - Gazpacho	L - Chinese Chicken Salad
Apple Tuna Salad with Croissants	Pita Bread with Sesame Seeds
Carrot Bars	D - Mary's Baked Fish
D - Lemon Chicken	Rosemary Potatoes
Vegetable Stuffed Potato	Broccoli in Orange Sauce
Green Beans with Dill	Italian Tomato Salad
Romaine and Mushroom Salad	Pineapple Prize Cake
Easy Fruit Dessert	

DAY THREE	DAY EIGHT
page 54 to 59	**page 82 to 86**
B - Blueberry Muffin Cake	B - Broiled Grapefruit
L - Seafood Salad	L - Vegetable Fritata
D - Grilled Beef Kabob	D - Roast Pork Tenderloin with Mustard Sauce
Pilaf Rice	Yvonne's Oven Potatoes
Baked Tomatoes	Stir Fry Vegetables
Spinach Salad	Sauteed Apples
Key Lime Pie	No Roll Cherry Pie

DAY FOUR	DAY NINE
page 60 to 64	**page 87 to 92**
B - Zucchini Muffins	B - Ham and Cheese Strata
L - Vegetable Pasta Salad	L - Ginger Fruit Salad
Grandma Church's Chocolate Chip Cake	D - Pepper Steak
D - Chicken Pina Colada	Egg Rolls
Steamed Rice	Steamed Rice
Snow Peas and Carrots	Cucumber Salad
Berries in Season	Fortune Cookies with Italian Ice

DAY FIVE	DAY TEN
page 65 to 70	**page 93 to 98**
B - One Eye Egg Surprise	B - Marty's Omelets
L - Moni's Chicken Salad a la Peach	L - Herbal Pasta Salad
D - Grilled Sword Fish	Sugar Cookies
Linguini Prima Vera	D - Shrimp Curry with Condiments
Lemon Bars	Oven Rice
	Bib Lettuce with Orange Vinaigrette
	Swedish Creme and Fresh Fruit

DAY ONE

BREAKFAST

FRUIT JUICE
ORANGE FRENCH TOAST

LUNCH

SAUTEED CHICKEN SALAD
RANCH DRESSING
PITA PARMESAN
NANNIE'S CHOCOLATE CHIP COOKIES

DINNER

FLORIDA FRIED FISH
TARTAR SAUCE
STUFFED SWEET POTATO
STEAMED BROCCOLI
HEARTS OF PALM SALAD

DESSERT

HOT RASPBERRY SUNDAE

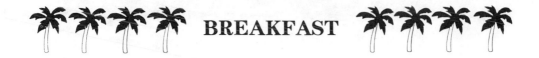
ORANGE FRENCH TOAST
Serves 4

This is easy, yet delightfully different!

2 eggs
¾ cup orange juice
2 T. sugar
8 slices firm textured bread
2 T. butter or margarine
3 T. confectioner's sugar
Dash of cinnamon
Maple syrup

1. Put eggs in pyrex pie pan and whisk gently.
2. Add orange juice and sugar and blend well.
3. Dip bread briefly into the egg mixture.
4. Melt margarine in large frying pan or electric skillet over medium/high heat.
5. Saute slices, turning once, until golden brown.
6. Mix confectioner's sugar with cinnamon and sprinkle over toast before serving.
7. Serve with maple syrup, slightly warmed.

Garnish with thin sliced fresh orange.

SAUTEED CHICKEN SALAD
Serves 4

This can be prepared in advance, refrigerated, and assembled at serving time.

½ head of romaine lettuce
½ head of iceberg lettuce
1 lg. red pepper
1 lg. green pepper
1 lg. yellow pepper
1 med. cucumber
2 med. tomatoes
1 15 oz. can of black beans
   (Frijoles Negro)
2 double breasts of skinless
   and boneless chicken
Italian seasoning (spices)
   to taste
Cooking spray
Low calorie ranch dressing

1. Wash and dry salad ingredients.
2. Break lettuce into small pieces.
3. Slice peppers, tomatoes and cucumbers into bite size pieces.
4. Drain and rinse black beans. Drain again.
5. Cut chicken into 1″ strips.
6. Spray frying pan with cooking spray. Season strips with Italian seasoning and saute about 2 minutes on each side over medium heat.
7. While the chicken is cooling, arrange lettuce and vegetables on individual plates. Arrange chicken strips on top of salad.
8. Sprinkle with black beans.
9. Serve dressing on the side.

PITA PARMESAN
Serves 4

8 lg. pita bread pockets
Melted butter
Garlic salt
Parmesan cheese

1. Preheat oven to 350 degrees.
2. Split pita in half and brush lightly with butter.
3. Sprinkle with garlic salt and Parmesan cheese.
4. Bake until crisp, about 15 minutes.

Serve in your favorite basket lined with a colorful napkin.

NANNIE'S CHOCOLATE CHIP COOKIES

Yields 4 dozen

These freeze well and are great to have on hand for snacks.

2½ cups flour
1 t. baking soda
1 cup butter or margarine
¼ cup sugar
¾ cup light brown sugar
1 t. vanilla
1 3½ oz. pkg. instant vanilla
 pudding
2 eggs
1 12 oz. pkg. semi-sweet
 chocolate chips

1. Mix flour and baking soda together.
2. Cream butter, sugars, vanilla and instant pudding mix.
3. Beat in eggs.
4. Add flour mixture and chocolate chips.
5. Drop by teaspoon full on ungreased cookie sheet.
6. Bake at 375 degrees for 6 - 8 minutes.

For variety, you can substitute butterscotch pudding for vanilla pudding.

FLORIDA FRIED FISH   Serves 4

This is a great way to fix your guests' catch of the day!

2 lbs. of any firm, non-oily
fish (grouper, red fish,
dolphin, snook)
2 eggs
1½ cups Italian seasoned
bread crumbs
½ cup vegetable oil
2 zip lock bags
Tartar sauce
Cocktail sauce
Lemon

1. Cut fish into serving size pieces.
2. Whisk two eggs and transfer to a zip lock bag. Add fish and coat with egg.
3. In another zip lock bag put bread crumbs. Shake fish in crumbs.
4. Cover bottom of skillet with ¾″ vegetable oil. Heat until very hot.
5. Heat oven to 225 degrees.
6. Fry a few pieces at a time so that the oil stays hot. When one side is golden brown, turn over.
7. Drain fried fish on paper lined plate.
8. Place plate in preheated oven for 10 - 15 minutes. This will keep the fish warm and crisp until serving time.
9. Serve with tartar sauce, and/or cocktail sauce and lemon.

For a tropical touch, garnish with fresh flowers.

TARTAR SAUCE
¼ cup mayonnaise
¼ cup non-fat yogurt
¼ cup sweet pickle relish
1 T. onion, chopped
½ t. lemon juice

1. Mix all ingredients and chill.

For variety, replace sweet relish with dill relish.

STUFFED SWEET POTATO

These can be made ahead of time and kept refrigerated.

4 med. sized sweet potatoes
3 T. brown sugar
3 T. cognac or brandy
3 T. butter or margarine
3 T. orange juice
¼ t. of cinnamon
4 T. walnuts or pecans,
   chopped

1. Bake sweet potatoes at 350 degrees until tender, about 1 hour.
2. When cool enough to handle, slice off the top of the potatoes lengthwise.
3. Scoop out pulp and mash. Save the potato shells.
4. Add brown sugar, cognac, butter and cinnamon. Add orange juice. If you are making these ahead of time, add more juice to keep them moist. Return to shell.
5. Top with chopped walnuts or pecans.
6. Heat in 350 degree oven for 15 minutes.

Keep them warm at 225 degrees while preparing the Florida Fried Fish.

STEAMED BROCCOLI

1 bunch broccoli
½ t. baking soda
Salt and pepper to taste

1. Wash and cut broccoli into flowerets.
2. Put an inch of water in pan and bring to a boil. Add baking soda. It will preserve the color of the broccoli.
3. Add broccoli, reduce heat to medium.
4. Cover and steam for about 3 minutes or until tender crisp.
5. Remove broccoli from pan, salt and pepper to taste.

Serve immediately!

HEARTS OF PALM SALAD

Serves 4

4 lg. leaves of Iceberg or
  Boston lettuce
1 15 oz. can hearts of palm
¼ of a red pepper
Vinaigrette dressing

1. Place lettuce on individual salad plates.
2. Cut hearts of palm in half lengthwise and place on lettuce.
3. Drizzle with your favorite vinaigrette dressing and garnish with thinly sliced red pepper.

 DESSERT

HOT RASPBERRY SUNDAE

Serves 4

1 qt. vanilla ice cream or
  frozen yogurt
1 10 oz. pkg. frozen
  raspberries
Canned or fresh whipping
  cream
Sugar wafers

1. Thaw raspberries and heat without boiling.
2. Put two scoops of ice cream or frozen yogurt into bowls or goblets.
3. Spoon warm sauce over ice cream.
4. Decorate with whipping cream and sugar wafers.
5. Serve immediately.

Can also be served with cold raspberry sauce.

DAY TWO

BREAKFAST

JUICE OR FRESH FRUIT OF YOUR CHOICE
BARB'S BREAKFAST CASSEROLE

LUNCH

GAZPACHO
APPLE TUNA SALAD WITH CROISSANTS
CARROT BARS

DINNER

LEMON CHICKEN
VEGETABLE STUFFED POTATOES
GREEN BEANS WITH DILL
ROMAINE AND MUSHROOM SALAD

DESSERT

EASY FRUIT DESSERT

BARB'S BREAKFAST CASSEROLE Serves 4

Can be assembled the night before and kept refrigerated. Bake just before serving.

1 16 oz. pkg. frozen hashbrown potatoes, defrosted
1½ c. shredded cheddar cheese
1 cup milk
1 cup cooked ham (or turkey ham) finely chopped
½ cup onions, sliced (green onions, optional)
½ t. salt
1 t. dry mustard
Dash cayenne pepper
5 eggs, beaten
Paprika

1. Line bottom of 12x17x2 pan with hashbrowns.
2. Mix all ingredients except eggs and paprika. Pour over the hashbrowns.
3. Beat eggs and pour over the mixture. Sprinkle with paprika.
4. Bake at 350 degrees for 40 - 45 minutes.

To add more zing, serve with salsa sauce.

GAZPACHO
Serves 4

Cool and refreshing!

1 cup tomatoes
½ cup green pepper
½ cup celery
½ cup cucumber
¼ cup onion
2 t. parsley, minced
1 t. chives, minced
1 sm. clove garlic, minced
2½ t. wine vinegar
2 T. olive oil
1 t. salt
¼ t. pepper
½ t. Worcestershire sauce
2 cups tomato juice
Croutons

1. Finely chop first five ingredients. May be chopped in food processor.
2. Combine all ingredients in glass bowl. Cover and chill thoroughly.
3. Serve in chilled bowls.
4. Top with croutons if desired.

APPLE TUNA SALAD
Serves 4

Tuna salad with a twist!

2 lg. apples (red delicious)
2 6.5 oz. cans tuna
   (in water)
6 T. lite mayonnaise
2 t. vinegar
3 t. dill
Pepper to taste
Lettuce leaves
4 croissants

1. Chop one apple into small pieces.
2. Add drained tuna and mix with mayonnaise.
3. Add vinegar, dill, pepper to taste.
4. Slice second apple.
5. Serve on lettuce leaves garnished with apple slices.
6. Pass croissants.

CARROT BARS

2 eggs
1 cup sugar
¾ cup oil
2 4.5 oz. jars carrot baby
   food
1 t. vanilla
1¼ cup flour
1 t. baking soda
1 t. cinnamon
1 t. salt
½ cup walnuts, chopped

1. Beat eggs, sugar and oil.
2. Add carrots and vanilla.
3. Sift flour, baking soda, cinnamon and salt.
4. Add egg mixture. Stir in chopped nuts.
5. Pour into greased and floured 9 x 13 pan.
6. Bake at 350 degrees for 25 - 35 minutes. Frost when cool.

FROSTING
3 oz. cream cheese
¼ cup butter or margarine
2 cups powdered sugar
1 t. vanilla

1. Mix cream cheese and butter until creamy.
2. Add sugar and vanilla.
3. Beat mixture until smooth. Frost bars.

Carrot bars can be made ahead of time and frozen.

LEMON CHICKEN
Serves 4

The chicken must be marinated one day before serving.

1 whole chicken, quartered
OR 2 whole chicken
breasts, split
1¼ cups fresh lemon juice
(about 5 lemons)
½ cup flour
1 t. paprika
Salt and pepper to taste
½ cup chicken broth
1¼ T. brown sugar
½ lemon, sliced
1½ t. Italian seasoning

1. Place the chicken pieces in a shallow dish.
2. Pour lemon juice over the chicken and marinate covered in the refrigerator overnight.
3. Preheat the oven to 375 degrees.
4. Drain the chicken, reserving the lemon juice.
5. Combine flour, paprika, salt and pepper.
6. Dredge chicken through the flour mixture and place skin side up in a shallow baking dish.
7. Bake the chicken for 40 minutes.
8. While the chicken is baking, blend the reserved lemon juice with broth and brown sugar. Add the lemon slices.
9. Pour this mixture over the chicken and sprinkle with Italian seasoning. Bake another 20 minutes, basting several times with pan juices.

This is delicious served hot, warm or cold.

VEGETABLE STUFFED POTATO   Serves 4

4 Baking Potatoes
2 T. margarine
1 cup chopped onion
1 cup shredded carrots
1 cup sliced mushrooms
¼ cup milk
1 T. lemon juice
1 t. Dijon mustard
1 t. salt
¼ t. pepper

1. Scrub potatoes, dry and prick with a fork.
2. Bake in a 425 degree oven for 55 - 60 minutes or until soft.
3. When the potatoes are done, cool to room temperature.
4. Carefully scoop out potatoes without breaking the skin. Set skin aside.
5. Meanwhile in medium saucepan melt margarine. Saute onion, carrots and mushrooms until soft.
6. In large bowl, whip potatoes. Add milk, lemon juice, mustard, salt and pepper. Beat until smooth. Stir in sauteed vegetables.
7. Spoon potato mixture into reserved skins.
8. Bake in a 350 degree oven 20 - 30 minutes until potatoes are heated through.

These can be assembled early in the day and heated before serving or substitute oven rice, page 97, if hurried.

GREEN BEANS WITH DILL   Serves 4

1 lb. fresh green beans
½ t. baking soda
1 t. butter or margarine
1 t. dill
Salt and pepper to taste

1. Wash and trim fresh green beans.
2. Bring water to a boil. Add baking soda. The baking soda will bring out the green color of the beans.
3. Add green beans, reduce heat, cover pot and cook beans for 3 - 4 minutes until tender but still crisp.
4. Drain beans. Dot with butter or margarine and sprinkle with dill. Add salt and pepper to taste.

ROMAINE AND MUSHROOM SALAD

Serves 4

1 head romaine lettuce
8 oz. mushrooms
1 sm. red onion

1. Wash and dry lettuce. Break into bite size pieces.
2. Wash, stem and slice mushrooms.
3. Slice onion and separate into rings.
4. Place into salad bowl and toss.
5. At serving time, pour dressing over salad. Toss gently until salad is coated thoroughly.

Serve with your favorite dressing. We particularly like red wine vinegar dressing.

 **DESSERT**

EASY FRUIT DESSERT

Serves 4

Light and refreshing!

1 cup seedless red grapes
1 cup seedless green grapes
1 4 oz. can mandarin
  oranges OR 1 fresh
  navel orange, sectioned
1 12 oz. can ginger ale
1 pint sherbet

1. Fill chilled dessert dishes with fruit mixture.
2. Pour ¼ of chilled ginger ale over each serving.
3. Top with 1 scoop of your favorite sherbet.
4. Serve at once.

DAY THREE

BREAKFAST

ORANGE JUICE
BLUEBERRY MUFFIN CAKE

LUNCH

SEAFOOD SALAD
ROLLS

DINNER

GRILLED BEEF KABOBS
PILAF RICE
BAKED TOMATOES
SPINACH SALAD

DESSERT

KEY LIME PIE

BLUEBERRY MUFFIN CAKE   Yields 12 servings

Can be made ahead of time and kept frozen.

2 T. fine, dry bread crumbs
2 cups flour
1 cup sugar
1 T. baking powder
½ t. baking soda
½ t. salt
½ t. cinnamon
1 cup fresh or frozen
   blueberries thawed and
   drained
2 eggs
⅓ cup orange juice
¼ cup margarine, softened
   at room temperature
8 oz. dairy sour cream
1 t. grated orange peel

TOPPING
¼ cup flour
¼ cup sugar
½ t. cinnamon
1½ T. margarine

1. Heat oven to 375 degrees. Grease 10″ spring form pan or 9″ square pan. Sprinkle with bread crumbs and set aside.
2. Spoon flour into measuring cup and level off.
3. In large bowl, combine flour, sugar, baking powder, baking soda, salt and cinnamon. Mix well.
4. Stir in blueberries. Beat eggs in medium size bowl. Add orange juice, margarine, sour cream and orange peel.
5. Add to blueberry mixture, stirring until dry ingredients are moistened.
6. In small bowl combine all crumb topping ingredients except margarine; mixing well. Slice margarine and add to mixture until it resembles coarse crumbs. Set aside.
7. Spoon batter into greased pan; sprinkle with crumb topping.
8. Bake in 375 degree oven for 35 - 45 minutes or until toothpick inserted comes out clean.
9. Cool for 10 minutes before removing from pan. Serve warm or cool.

It's easy to prepare even though the directions seem lengthy.

SEAFOOD SALAD
Serves 4

Prepare early in the day to blend flavors!

1 lb. imitation crab meat
¼ cup green pepper
¼ cup red pepper
¼ cup yellow pepper
2 T. onion, finely minced
¼ cup lite mayonnaise
Pepper to taste
2 med. tomatoes
1 med. cucumber
Fresh parsley
Lettuce
Rolls

1. Shred crab meat.
2. Finely chop peppers.
3. Mix the first seven ingredients and chill at least 4 hours.
4. Serve with tomato and cucumber slices.
5. Sprinkle with chopped fresh parsley.
6. Serve on a bed of lettuce.
7. Pass the rolls.

GRILLED BEEF KABOBS   Serves 4

If you don't have a grill available, broil kabobs 4 - 5 minutes on each side.

1 lb. eye round roast
1 med. green pepper
1 med. red pepper
1 lg. red onion
8 lg. mushrooms
1 bottle Teriyaki Baste & Glaze

1. Cut beef into 1½" square chunks.
2. Seed and cut peppers into 1" squares.
3. Quarter onion and cut each quarter in half.
4. Wash mushrooms and par boil for two minutes.
5. Thread vegetables and beef alternately on skewers.
6. Place skewers on large platter. Pour Teriyaki Baste & Glaze over kabobs and let stand at room temperature for 30 min.
7. Grill kabobs over medium-hot fire for 10 to 12 minutes or until done to your liking.

You can also use shrimp, scallops, chicken, lamb or pork tenderloin chunks.

If you don't have metal skewers, use 10" bamboo skewers. They are inexpensive and readily available at most supermarkets. Wet them and thread the meat and vegetables tightly to prevent burning.

PILAF RICE

1 cup long grain white rice
3 T. margarine
¼ cup chopped onion
2½ cups hot water
1 t. marjoram
1 t. rosemary
½ t. savory
1 t. instant chicken bouillon
½ t. coarsely ground pepper

1. Wash rice several times and drain.
2. In electric frying pan or stove top frying pan melt margarine.
3. Add rice and saute over medium heat until evenly brown (about 5 min.).
4. Add onion, spices and hot water. Cook on low until water is absorbed and rice is cooked. (About 20 min.) Check to see if more water is needed.

This can be made ahead of time - in fact the flavors blend better if made ahead. When reheating, separate rice with fork and add a little more water if necessary.

BAKED TOMATOES

4 tomatoes
¹/₃ cup seasoned bread
   crumbs
1 T. Parmesan cheese,
   grated
¼ t. salt
Dash of pepper
1 T. butter

1. Cut tops off tomatoes. Cut in half widthwise. You may have to cut a little off the bottom so they'll sit upright on a cookie sheet or small flat pan.
2. Mix bread crumbs, Parmesan cheese, salt and pepper.
3. Sprinkle over tomatoes.
4. Dot with butter.
5. Bake for 15 - 20 minutes at 350 degrees.

This makes a lovely garnish for other meals as well.

SPINACH SALAD

10 oz. spinach
1 lg. tomato
6 bacon strips
2 t. onion, grated
1 t. salt
½ t. pepper
2 t. Dijon mustard
1½ t. red wine vinegar
½ cup olive oil
¼ t. lemon juice
8 oz. mushrooms, sliced thin
5 radishes, thinly sliced

1. Wash and dry spinach. Cut tomato into small wedges. Fry bacon crispy, drain and crumble.
2. Mix onion, salt, pepper and mustard.
3. Moisten this paste with vinegar.
4. Whisk oil into mixture until it has the consistency of mayonnaise.
5. Stir in lemon juice.
6. Place spinach in a bowl and toss with dressing, tomato, mushrooms and radishes.
7. Sprinkle with bacon bits.

KEY LIME PIE

Makes 2 pies, 8 servings each

Prepare earlier in the day. Serve one, freeze one!

2 prepared graham cracker crusts
4 egg yolks
1 14 oz. can sweetened condensed milk
2/3 cup KEY LIME JUICE, fresh if possible or bottled
4 egg whites
1 sm. container of non-dairy whipped topping
1 fresh lime, sliced thin

1. Bake crusts for 5 minutes at 350 degrees. Remove from oven.
2. Beat egg yolks in medium bowl. Add sweetened condensed milk and mix.
3. Add key lime juice **very slowly** while beating constantly.
4. Beat egg whites until stiff. Fold into egg yolk mixture.
5. Fold in non-dairy whipped topping.
6. Pour into crusts. Chill for 4 hours.

Garnish with whipped topping and lime slices.

Garnish: After you have sliced lime thinly, cut each slice half-way. Bend slice where you cut it in opposite direction, so each slice can be placed upright on top of the pie. Arrange slices in a circle appr. 1 inch from edge of pie. Fill whipped topping into pastry bag and garnish edge of pie.

DAY FOUR

BREAKFAST

HALF GRAPEFRUIT
ZUCCHINI MUFFINS

LUNCH

VEGETABLE PASTA SALAD
SLICED TOMATOES
ROLLS
GRANDMA CHURCH'S CHOCOLATE CHIP CAKE

DINNER

CHICKEN PINA COLADA
STEAMED RICE
SNOW PEAS AND CARROTS

DESSERT

BERRIES IN SEASON

ZUCCHINI MUFFINS   Yields 24 muffins or 2 loaves

Freeze what you don't use!

3 eggs
1 cup yellow raisins
1 cup sugar
1 cup brown sugar
¼ t. baking powder
2 t. baking soda
1 cup oil
1 T. vanilla
1 T. cinnamon
1 t. salt
1 cup walnuts, chopped
2 cups zucchini, grated
2 cups flour

1. Beat eggs until foamy. This is very important.
2. Add all other ingredients to eggs and mix.
3. Grease and flour loaf pans or muffin tins lightly. Pour in batter.
4. Bake at 350 degrees for 20 minutes for muffins or 55 - 60 minutes for loaves.
5. Check center of muffins or loaves with a toothpick for doneness.

VEGETABLE PASTA SALAD

Serves 4

1 12 oz. pkg. curly pasta
¼ cup lite mayonnaise
¼ cup non-fat plain yogurt
1 cup grated Parmesan
   cheese
¼ cup red wine vinegar
Juice of ½ med. lemon
1 4 oz. jar pimientos
1 2-½ oz. can black olives,
   sliced
1 cup frozen peas, thawed
½ cup fresh parsley

1. Cook pasta according to directions and cool.
2. Mix mayonnaise, yogurt, Parmesan cheese, vinegar and lemon juice.
3. Add pimientos, sliced olives, peas and chopped parsley.
4. Toss with half of mayonnaise/yogurt mixture and refrigerate.
5. At serving time add remaining dressing and toss.

If desired, shrimp, chicken or pepperoni can be added to the pasta. May be served in a bowl or on a bed of lettuce on individual plates. Garnish with sliced tomatoes. Serve with fresh rolls.

GRANDMA CHURCH'S CHOCOLATE CHIP CAKE

Serves 12

This is an all time favorite with Grandma Church's family!

1 3.5 oz. box chocolate
   pudding (not instant)
2 cups milk
1 box plain chocolate cake
   mix
1 6 oz. pkg. chocolate chips,
   semi-sweet

1. Prepare chocolate pudding as directed on the package and let cool.
2. Add the cake mix and stir.
3. Transfer mixture to a greased 9 x 13 baking pan.
4. Sprinkle with chocolate chips and bake in preheated 350 degree oven for 25 - 30 minutes.

Keep these ingredients on your shelf and you can serve cake in 45 minutes. You can add chopped nuts if desired.

CHICKEN PINA COLADA   Serves 4

Wait until you taste this one. Easy and so delicious.

8 half chicken breast,
    skinless and boneless
Salt and pepper to taste
1 8 oz. can Coco Lopez
    Cream of Coconut
¼ cup grated coconut

1. Trim chicken and place in baking pan Season with salt and pepper to taste.
2. Pour cream of coconut over the chicken.
3. Bake at 350 degrees for 35 - 45 minutes.
4. Sprinkle with grated coconut. Bake until coconut is golden brown.

Garnish with pineapple rings and parsley.

STEAMED RICE   Serves 4

1 cup long grain rice
1¾ cup water

1. Place rice in heavy sauce pan. Wash and drain several times to remove excess starch.
2. Add water and bring to a rapid boil for 3 - 4 minutes until holes begin to form on the surface of the rice. Cover and turn heat to low.
3. Continue cooking for 20 minutes. Turn off heat and allow to remain in pot, covered, for 10 additional minutes.

SNOW PEAS AND CARROTS Serves 4

¾ lbs. carrots
¼ lb. snow peas, fresh or
  frozen
2 T. butter or margarine
1 T. sesame seeds
½ t. garlic, minced
2 T. chives, chopped (or
  green onions)
1 T. soy sauce

1. Peel, trim and slice carrots into julienne strips, 1½" long.
2. Wash and trim snow peas.
3. Place carrots in sauce pan with water and cover. Bring to a boil. Simmer for 4 minutes.
4. In large skillet melt butter; add sesame seeds. Cook until seeds are lightly toasted, stirring frequently.
5. Add garlic, carrots and snow peas, chives and soy sauce. Saute while stirring for 1 minute.

 DESSERT

BERRIES IN SEASON Serves 4

3 cups of berries in season
  (frozen if fresh are not
  available)

1. Wash and drain berries.
2. Divide between 4 serving dishes.
3. Serve with one of the following suggestions.

1. 1 cup vanilla yogurt mixed with ½ cup mashed strawberries and 1 t. lemon juice.

2. 1 cup non-fat yogurt mixed with 2 T. orange juice and 1 t. grated orange rind.

3. Serve frozen berries over a slice of frozen pound cake and top with whipping cream or one of the yogurt toppings.

DAY FIVE

BREAKFAST

FRESH MELON
ONE EYE EGG SURPRISE

LUNCH

MONI'S CHICKEN SALAD A LA PEACH
FRENCH BREAD

DINNER

GRILLED SWORD FISH
LINGUINI PRIMA VERA
CRUNCHY BREAD

DESSERT

LEMON BARS

ONE EYE EGG SURPRISE

Serves 4

4 slices of bread
Cooking spray
3 T. butter or margarine
4 eggs
Salt and pepper to taste

1. Cut holes in the center of each slice of bread using the opening of a small juice glass.
2. Butter bread slices on both sides.
3. Spray skillet or electric frying pan with cooking spray.
4. Add butter or margarine to pan over medium heat. Add bread slice.
5. Break one egg and put in center of the bread slice. Fry briefly, then flip and fry on other side until desired doneness. Add more butter if needed.

MONI'S CHICKEN SALAD A LA PEACH

Serves 4

Try this recipe with light cream cheese or plain yogurt instead of regular cream cheese.

2 double chicken breast, skinless and boneless
1 29 oz. can peach halves
4 oz. cream cheese
4 T. peach syrup
2 - 3 t. curry powder
1 t. lemon juice
Sugar and salt to taste
Boston lettuce
Parsley

1. Poach chicken breast, cool and cut into ½" cubes.
2. Drain peaches, reserving syrup.
3. Puree 4 peach halves with cream cheese and syrup until smooth and creamy.
4. Add curry, lemon juice, sugar and salt.
5. Add chicken to peach mixture and coat well.
6. Arrange chicken salad on a bed of lettuce, garnish with remaining peach halves and parsley.

Keep these ingredients stocked and you are minutes away from a delicious treat! Serve with crunchy French bread.

GRILLED SWORD FISH
WITH TERIYAKI
Serves 4

You can also use fresh tuna instead of sword fish. Cut cooking time in half so tuna is rare in the middle.

**4 sword fish steaks
 (¾″ thick)**
**1 bottle Teriyaki Baste &
 Glaze**
Fresh parsley, chopped

1. Preheat grill on high for about 15 minutes.
2. Coat sword fish steaks with Teriyaki Baste & Glaze.
3. Grill for 4 - 5 minutes on each side or until done.
4. Remove from grill and sprinkle with parsley. Serve immediately.

LINGUINI PRIMA VERA

Serves 4

Can be assembled ahead of time and refrigerated.

4 oz. linguini
1 med. green pepper
2 med. zucchini
4 med. tomatoes
¼ cup fresh parsley
⅓ cup butter or margarine
⅓ cup onion, chopped
½ cup Parmesan cheese,
  grated
½ cup Swiss cheese, grated
Salt and pepper to taste
Oregano to taste

1. Break linguini into 1" pieces. Cook and drain.
2. Seed and thinly slice green pepper.
3. Cut zucchini into spears.
4. Cut tomatoes into wedges.
5. Chop the parsley.
6. Melt butter in skillet and saute onions for about 5 minutes.
7. Add green peppers and saute for a few more minutes.
8. Place half of the pasta on bottom of buttered 2 quart casserole.
9. Place half of the vegetables and cheese on top of the pasta reserving ¼ cup of the Parmesan cheese for topping.
10. Repeat layer.
11. Add seasonings to taste.
12. Bake at 350 degrees for 30 - 40 minutes. Do not overcook.
13. Top with remaining ¼ cup Parmesan cheese.

Serve with crunchy Italian bread.

LEMON BARS

Yields 16 bars

CRUST
½ cup butter or margarine
1 cup flour
¼ cup powdered sugar

1. Mix crust ingredients and pat on bottom of 9″ square pan.
2. Bake at 350 degrees for 15 minutes.

Flour hands before patting dough into pan.

TOPPING
2 T. flour
¾ cup sugar
½ t. baking powder
2 eggs, beaten
2 T. lemon juice
Grated rind of a small
   lemon

1. Sift flour, sugar and baking powder.
2. Add eggs, juice and rind.
3. Pour on top of baked crust and bake at 350 degrees for 25 minutes.
4. Let cool and cut into squares.

Sprinkle with powdered sugar. Freezes well!

DAY SIX

BREAKFAST

FRUIT JUICE
BAGELS OR ENGLISH MUFFINS WITH
ORANGE CREAM CHEESE SPREAD

LUNCH

CAESAR SALAD
FRENCH BREAD

DINNER

GRILLED BUTTERFLIED LEG OF LAMB A LA BETTY
BOILED NEW POTATOES
CAULIFLOWER SCRAMBLE
ROMAINE AND MANDARIN ORANGE SALAD

DESSERT

GRAPES IN A GOBLET

 **BREAKFAST**

ORANGE CREAM CHEESE SPREAD
Serves 4

1 orange
1 8 oz. pkg. of cream cheese
1 T. honey
1 T. pecans
4 bagels or English muffins

1. Grate orange rind.
2. Peel, seed and chop orange.
3. Soften cream cheese.
4. Chop pecans.
5. Combine all ingredients, mix well.
6. Serve on bagels or English muffins.

This can also be served on crackers for hors d'oeuvres.

 **LUNCH**

CAESAR SALAD
Serves 4

1 head romaine lettuce
2 - 3 cloves of garlic, minced
2 T. red wine vinegar
Juice of ½ medium lemon
1 2 oz. tin anchovies, finely
 chopped
½ t. Dijon mustard
Coarsely ground pepper to
 taste
1 egg
½ - 1 t. Worcestershire sauce
⅓ cup olive oil
⅓ cup Parmesan cheese
2 cups croutons

1. Wash lettuce and dry very well.
2. Pour red wine vinegar over the garlic in large wooden bowl. Marinate for about 5 minutes.
3. Add lemon juice, whisk in anchovies, mustard, pepper, egg, Worcestershire sauce, olive oil, and Parmesan cheese.
4. Serve over chilled romaine lettuce and toss lightly with croutons.

For a heartier salad, add smoked chicken, grilled chicken, smoked salmon, smoked fish, smoked shrimp or smoked scallops.

GRILLED BUTTERFLIED LEG OF LAMB A LA BETTY

Serves 4

1 leg of lamb, boned and
    butterflied
2 T. fresh parsley
1 cup onion
½ cup olive oil
¾ cup dry white wine
2 T. fresh lemon juice
1 t. oregano
3 crumbled bay leaves
3 garlic cloves
1 t. salt
Mint jelly

1. Have the butcher bone and butterfly a leg of lamb. Remove most of the fat and all of the skin.
2. Chop parsley and thinly slice onion.
3. Mix all remaining ingredients. Marinate the lamb, covered, in the refrigerator for several hours, turning occasionally.
4. Let the meat come to room temperature before grilling.
5. Grill on medium/high for about 15 minutes on each side. (You and/or the grill cook must make the decision as to when it is done.) There should be some rare, some pink and some well done.
6. Carve thin slices, perpendicularly as you would a steak.
7. Serve with mint jelly.

This can also be roasted in the oven at 400 degrees for about 35   45 minutes. Allow more time and check for desired doneness.

BOILED NEW POTATOES

Serves 4

12 small new potatoes
Butter or margarine
Fresh parsley

1. Scrub and boil potatoes until tender (15 - 20 minutes).
2. Drain, shake potatoes in dry pan over burner to dry the skins.
3. Serve garnished with fresh parsley and pass butter or margarine for those who wish to have it.

CAULIFLOWER SCRAMBLE

Serves 4

2 10 oz. boxes cauliflower
   flowerets, frozen, in
   cheese sauce
2 T. onion
1 med. zucchini
1 T. margarine or butter
1 med. tomato
½ t. salt
Pepper to taste
½ t. dill weed (optional)

1. Cook cauliflower according to package directions.
2. Chop onion and slice zucchini. Cut tomatoes into 8 wedges.
3. In medium size skillet saute zucchini and onion until tender.
4. Stir in cauliflower, tomatoes and spices and heat thoroughly.
5. Can be assembled ahead and reheated before serving.

ROMAINE AND MANDARIN ORANGE SALAD

Serves 4

1 head romaine lettuce
1 sm. red onion
1 8 oz. can mandarin
    oranges, drained
1 4 oz. pkg. sliced almonds

1. Wash, dry and chill lettuce. Cut onion into rings.
2. Add mandarin oranges and toss.
3. Prepare dressing and pour over salad before serving.
4. Sprinkle with almonds.

HONEY MUSTARD
DRESSING
½ cup olive oil
¼ cup lemon juice
½ t. salt
1 t. Worcestershire sauce
1 T. Dijon mustard
1 T. honey
¼ t. pepper

1. Mix ingredients, chill.
2. Shake vigorously before serving.

You may substitute an olive oil and vinegar dressing for variety.

 **DESSERT**

GRAPES IN A GOBLET

Serves 4

1 cup red seedless grapes
1 cup green seedless grapes
⅓ cup honey
2 T. brandy or cognac
2 T. lemon juice
4 T. sour cream or plain
    yogurt

1. Put grapes in glass bowl.
2. Mix honey, brandy and lemon juice and pour over grapes.
3. Stir well and refrigerate several hours. Stir occasionally.
4. To serve, place grapes in pretty goblets and top each portion with 1 T. sour cream or yogurt.

DAY SEVEN

BREAKFAST

FRUIT JUICE
APPLE PANCAKES WITH SYRUP

LUNCH

CHINESE CHICKEN SALAD
PITA BREAD WITH SESAME SEEDS

DINNER

MARY'S BAKED FISH
ROSEMARY POTATOES
BROCCOLI IN ORANGE SAUCE
ITALIAN TOMATO SALAD

DESSERT

PINEAPPLE PRIZE CAKE

APPLE PANCAKES

Serves 4

Pancake mix of your choice
2 med. apples
   (Red Delicious)
Oil
Butter or margarine
Powdered sugar
Maple syrup, warmed

1. Prepare pancake batter according to directions for 4.
2. Peel, core and slice apples.
3. Heat skillet or griddle.
4. Melt butter and oil over medium/ high heat.
5. Saute apple slices for about 1 minute on each side.
6. Arrange a few slices at a time and pour pancake batter on top of it.
7. Bake pancakes as usual.

Sprinkle powdered sugar on pancakes and serve with butter and warmed maple syrup.

CHINESE CHICKEN SALAD   Serves 4

This is a wonderfully light and flavorful meal. If you keep some cooked chicken in your freezer, this salad can be made in minutes.

2 double chicken breasts
2 cups fresh bean sprouts
2 T. soy sauce
1 T. white vinegar
1 T. sesame oil
   (no substitute)
½ t. tabasco sauce or to taste
½ t. sugar

1. Poach and cool chicken. Remove skin and fat, chill.
2. Coarsely shred the cooked chicken breasts.
3. Wash and drain bean sprouts.
4. In a mixing bowl combine soy sauce, vinegar, sesame oil, tabasco and sugar.
5. Place the shredded chicken in a serving bowl, add the bean sprouts and dressing. Stir and serve.

Garnish with sliced cucumbers and cherry tomatoes, accompanied by a slice of cantaloupe.

PITA BREAD WITH SESAME SEEDS   Serves 4

4 white pita pocket breads
Butter or margarine
Sesame seeds

1. Preheat oven to 350 degrees.
2. Cut pita pockets in half. With sharp knife, cut around edges to separate. You should have 4 half circles from each pita bread.
3. Spread butter or margarine on inside of pita bread.
4. Sprinkle with sesame seeds.
5. Place on baking sheet, butter side up.
6. Bake at 350 degrees until golden brown, about 10 - 15 minutes.

 DINNER

MARY'S BAKED FISH   Serves 4

If you and your guests are seafood lovers, you may want to prepare 2½ pounds of fillet.

Juice of a small lemon
2 lbs. fish fillet (grouper or
   red snapper)
¼ cup non-fat plain yogurt
¼ cup lite mayonnaise
¼ cup Parmesan cheese
1 T. red wine vinegar
3 drops tabasco sauce
6 green onions, sliced

1. Squeeze lemon over fish fillet and marinate for 10 minutes.
2. Preheat oven to 350 degrees.
3. Mix yogurt, mayonnaise, Parmesan cheese, vinegar and tabasco. Add ¾ of the green onions.
4. Place fish fillets in a baking dish and pour sauce over it.
5. Place in preheated oven and bake for 10 - 15 minutes depending on the thickness of the fish. Test with fork for doneness.
6. Sprinkle with remaining green onions.

This is a wonderful blend of flavors! Garnish platter with thinly sliced lemon and parsley.

ROSEMARY POTATOES   Serves 4

Cooking spray
4 cups thinly sliced or cubed
   potatoes with skins
2 T. olive oil
1 T. rosemary
Salt and pepper to taste
1 T. water

1. Spray baking dish with cooking spray.
2. Place potatoes in pan.
3. Sprinkle with olive oil, rosemary, salt and pepper.
4. Add water and toss well.
5. Cover pan and bake at 350 degrees for 30 - 35 minutes or until tender, turning once after 15 minutes.

BROCCOLI IN ORANGE SAUCE   Serves 4

A new twist for broccoli!

1 lb. fresh broccoli
1 navel orange
¹⁄₃ cup orange juice
½ T. sugar
1 t. cornstarch
Dash ground ginger

1. Wash and trim broccoli. Remove flowerets from stem and set aside.
2. Peel and section the orange.
3. Slice stem into ¼″ rounds and put into 1½ quart pan. Place flowerets on top in 1″ of water, cover and bring to a boil. Cook over medium/high heat for 1-2 minutes. Drain.
4. Add orange sections to broccoli and heat through. Do not overcook.
5. In a small sauce pan blend orange juice, sugar, cornstarch and ginger. Pour over broccoli, heat and stir until thickened.

Fresh asparagus, without orange sauce, would also blend well with this meal.

ITALIAN TOMATO SALAD   Serves 4

Can be made ahead of time.

4 lg. vine ripe tomatoes
1 t. oregano
1 sm. red onion
1 t. salt
4 leaves fresh basil OR
1 t. dried basil
2 T. olive oil

1. Cut tomatoes into wedges and place in bowl.
2. Add oregano, sliced red onion, salt, basil and olive oil.
3. Toss and refrigerate.

You can also add cucumbers and peppers.

PINEAPPLE PRIZE CAKE   Yields 8 servings

Can be prepared a day in advance.

1 10¾ oz. frozen pound cake
⅓ cup pineapple juice AND
½ t. almond extract
1 16 oz. can crushed
  pineapple, drain and
  reserve juice
4 oz. non-dairy whipped
  topping
¼ cup instant vanilla
  pudding mix
¼ cup sliced almonds,
  toasted

1. Cut the cake lengthwise into thirds.
2. Mix pineapple juice and almond extract. Brush slices with this mixture.
3. Combine drained pineapple, whipped topping and pudding mix. Blend well.
4. Place bottom layer of cake on pretty serving dish.
5. Spread one third of this mixture over the bottom layer of cake. Do the same with second and top layer.
6. To toast almonds, place them on aluminum foil in 350 degree oven. Brown on both sides, turning frequently.
7. Sprinkle top with toasted almonds.

Have these ingredients ready on your shelf and/or freezer. You are only minutes away from a tasty dessert.

Chocolate lovers might want to try this pound cake version!

PARTY POUND CAKE   Yields 8 servings

1 10¾ oz. frozen pound cake
¼ cup orange marmalade
4 T. orange juice
1 can prepared chocolate
  frosting

1. Slice pound cake lengthwise into thirds.
2. Place bottom slice on serving plate.
3. Sprinkle 2 T orange juice on bottom layer and spread chocolate frosting on top of it.
4. Place second layer on top and sprinkle remaining orange juice on it. Spread marmalade on second layer.
5. Top with third layer and frost as you would a cake. Chill 4 hours.

DAY EIGHT

BREAKFAST

BROILED GRAPEFRUIT
CROISSANTS WITH HONEY AND JAM

LUNCH

VEGETABLE FRITATA
SOUR DOUGH ROLLS

DINNER

ROAST PORK TENDERLOIN WITH MUSTARD SAUCE
YVONNE'S OVEN POTATOES
STIR FRY VEGETABLES
SAUTEED APPLES

DESSERT

NO ROLL CHERRY PIE

 **BREAKFAST**

BROILED GRAPEFRUIT
Serves 4

2 grapefruit
2 T. butter or margarine
6 T. brown sugar

1. Cut grapefruit in half and around sections.
2. Melt butter with sugar until dissolved.
3. Drizzle butter/sugar mixture over cut side.
4. Broil until hot and bubbly (about 1½ minutes).
5. Garnish with strawberries and mint leaves, if available.
6. Serve at once.

This also makes a wonderfully light dessert.

 LUNCH

VEGETABLE FRITATA
Serves 4

2 T. butter
1 16 oz. frozen vegetables, diced OR
4 cups fresh vegetables, cut into ½″ cubes
8 eggs
2 T. milk
½ t. salt
¼ t. pepper
Sour dough rolls

1. Melt butter in frying pan.
2. Add vegetables, cover and cook for 3 minutes over medium/high heat, stirring 2 - 3 times.
3. Mix eggs, milk, salt and pepper in medium bowl.
4. Add to vegetables and cook covered over medium heat for 6 - 8 minutes until set.
5. Serve with rolls.

Any combination of vegetables works well. It's a great way to use up leftover vegetables.

 **DINNER**

PORK TENDERLOIN
WITH MUSTARD SAUCE Serves 4

Both of these sauces are wonderful. If you can't decide which one to use, make them both!

1 lb. pork tenderloin

1. Wash pork tenderloin and pat dry with paper towel.

MUSTARD SAUCE
½ **cup Dijon mustard**
2 t. **dry mustard**
1 T. **parsley flakes**
1 t. **dried thyme**
½ t. **ground black pepper**

2. Mix mustard and herbs and spread evenly on all sides of the pork.
3. Bake at 350 degrees for 40 minutes.
4. Slice and serve with extra sauce.

Slice the pork and arrange it on a large platter with parsley and cherry tomatoes.

APRICOT GLAZE
4 T. **apricot jam**
3 t. **dry Madeira wine**
2 t. **Dijon mustard**
2 t. **honey**
¼ t. **minced ginger**

1. In small saucepan combine all ingredients.
2. Heat over medium until mixture is smooth.
3. Spread evenly on all sides of tenderloin.
4. Proceed as 3 and 4 above.

This is also delicious prepared on your grill. Preheat grill on medium/high and grill tenderloin, turning frequently, for about 20 - 30 minutes.

YVONNE'S POTATOES

Serves 4

4 T. margarine
4 lg. potatoes
¼ cup grated Parmesan
   cheese
2 T. flour
Salt, pepper, paprika to
   taste

1. Melt margarine in 9 x 9 baking dish.
2. Peel the potatoes and cut into bite size pieces.
3. Put remaining ingredients in a zip lock bag.
4. Shake potatoes in cheese mixture coating well.
5. Place potatoes in baking dish and bake at 350 degrees, turning once, for 40 minutes until brown.

Crisp and zesty!

STIR FRIED VEGETABLES

Serves 4

1 med. red pepper
1 lg. zucchini
2 med. yellow squash
2 carrots, thinly sliced
1 cup onions, sliced
1½ T. vegetable oil
2 cloves garlic, minced
1 T. water
½ t. salt
¼ t. pepper
1 t. sugar
Soy sauce to taste

1. Cut pepper into bite size squares.
2. Slice zucchini and yellow squash.
3. Heat oil in frying pan or wok over high heat.
4. Add garlic, stir and immediately add vegetables to the pan. Stir fry for 2 minutes.
5. Add 1 T water, cover and steam for 2 more minutes.
6. Season with salt, pepper, sugar and soy sauce.

If you have mushrooms on hand, they make a nice addition.

SAUTEED APPLES

Serves 4

4 sm. apples
1 T. butter or margarine
1 t. cinnamon
1 T. brown sugar

1. Peel, core and slice apples.
2. Melt butter with cinnamon and brown sugar over med. heat.
3. Saute apples for 1 minute on each side.

If you want to slice the apples ahead of time, sprinkle them with lemon juice after slicing.

 **DESSERT**

NO ROLL CHERRY PIE

Yields 8 servings

CRUST
½ cup butter or margarine
1 T. sugar
1 cup flour

1. Melt butter and sugar in a saucepan.
2. Remove from heat.
3. Add flour. Stir until it forms a ball.
4. Press into bottom and sides of a 9″ pie pan.

FILLING
1 15 oz. can cherry pie
    filling

TOPPING
1 egg
½ cup sugar
¼ cup flour
¼ cup milk

1. In a small bowl, beat egg and sugar. Blend in flour and milk and stir until smooth.
2. Pour pie filling onto crust and spoon on topping
3. Bake at 350 degrees for 50 - 60 minutes.
4. Cool before removing from pan.

This is delicious no matter what kind of fruit filling you use!

DAY NINE

BREAKFAST

FRUIT JUICE
HAM AND CHEESE STRATA

LUNCH

GINGER FRUIT SALAD
WITH COTTAGE CHEESE OR YOGURT

DINNER

PEPPER STEAK
EGG ROLLS
STEAMED RICE
CUCUMBER SALAD

DESSERT

FORTUNE COOKIES AND ITALIAN ICE OR SHERBET
JASMINE TEA

HAM AND CHEESE STRATA

Serves 4

Must be assembled the night before!

½ cup butter or margarine
½ loaf French bread
½ lb. cheddar cheese, grated
2 cups cubed ham (turkey, shrimp or crab meat can be substituted)
5 eggs
1½ cups milk
Dash dry mustard
Salt and pepper to taste
Paprika
½ cup green olives, sliced

1. Butter a 9 x 12 casserole. Slice bread, butter each side and cut into cubes.
2. Spread buttered bread cubes on bottom of casserole.
3. Sprinkle grated cheese on top of bread cubes.
4. Top with ham cubes.
5. Mix eggs, milk, mustard, salt and pepper and pour over other ingredients.
6. Sprinkle with paprika and sliced olives.
7. Cover and refrigerate overnight.
8. Bake at 350 degrees for 45 - 55 minutes until set.
9. Cut in squares and serve.

GINGER FRUIT SALAD

Serves 4

1 lg. apple
2 navel oranges
2 med. peaches
1 cup strawberries
2 Kiwi fruits
2 t. lemon juice

1. Wash, core and coarsely chop apple.
2. Peel and section oranges.
3. Wash and slice peaches.
4. Wash and remove hulls from strawberries. Halve berries and add to salad.
5. Peel and slice kiwis.
6. Sprinkle lemon juice over fruit and toss gently.

GINGER DRESSING
1 cup vanilla yogurt
2 t. brown sugar
¼ t. ground ginger
2 T. orange juice

1. Mix all ingredients and blend well.
2. Pour ginger dressing over salad just before serving or serve on the side.

Serve on lettuce leaves with a scoop of cottage cheese or a dollop of yogurt. Sprinkle with chopped walnuts, if desired.

PEPPER STEAK
Serves 4

Don't be scared off by the lengthy instructions. It's easy to prepare and a sure hit with your company.

1 lb. flank steak
1 T. dry sherry wine
3 T. soy sauce
1 t. sugar
2 t. cornstarch
1 med. green pepper
1 med. red pepper
1 clove garlic, finely minced
1 T. vegetable oil
3 T. vegetable oil
4 slices fresh ginger peeled,
    1″ x ⅛″

1. Cut flank steak into very thin slices. Meat is easier to slice if partially frozen.
2. In a large bowl, mix wine, soy sauce, sugar and cornstarch. Add steak slices and mix to coat them thoroughly.
3. Marinate in refrigerator up to six hours. (It may also be cooked at once.)
4. Seed peppers and cut into 1″ squares.
5. Place oil, garlic, ginger root and peppers within easy reach.
6. Heat wok over high heat for 1 minute. (If you don't have a wok, a large heavy skillet will do.)
7. Add 1 T. vegetable oil. Heat 30 seconds.
8. Add peppers to hot oil and stir fry until tender but still crisp, about 3 minutes. Scoop out with slotted spoon and set aside.
9. Add remaining 3 T. oil to wok and heat.
10. Add ginger and garlic and a few seconds later, add the steak. Stir fry over high heat for 2 minutes or until there is no red showing. Add peppers and cook 1 additional minute.
11. Remove ginger slices. Serve immediately with steamed rice.

EGG ROLLS

Prepare 2 large frozen shrimp egg rolls per person according to package directions. The shrimp flavor blends well with the pepper steak.

STEAMED RICE

Serves 4

1 cup long grain rice
1¾ cup water

1. Wash and drain rice several times to remove excess starch.
2. Place rice in heavy sauce pan and add water. Bring to a rapid boil for 3 - 4 minutes until holes begin to form on the surface of the rice. Cover and turn heat to low.
3. Continue cooking for 20 minutes. Turn off heat and allow to remain in pot, covered, for 10 additional minutes.

CUCUMBER SALAD

Serves 4

2 lg. cucumbers
1 T. soy sauce
1 T. red wine vinegar
1 T. sugar
½ t. tabasco
1 T. sesame oil
(NO SUBSTITUTE)

1. Peel cucumbers. Cut in half lengthwise. Scoop out seeds with a spoon.
2. Cut into half circle slices about ¼" thick and chill.
3. Mix next 5 ingredients together for dressing.
4. Pour dressing over cucumbers when ready to serve. Toss and coat well.

Sesame oil is available in the Oriental section of most grocery stores.

 **DESSERT**

FORTUNE COOKIES
ITALIAN ICE
JASMINE TEA

Place 2 scoops Italian ice (or sherbet) in each serving bowl. Decorate with mint leaves or a strawberry. Pass fortune cookies and serve Jasmine tea. Be sure to read your fortunes out loud. It makes for lively after dinner conversation!

DAY TEN

BREAKFAST

SLICED ORANGES
MARTY'S OMELETS
TOAST AND JELLY

LUNCH

HERBAL PASTA SALAD
SLICED TOMATOES
SUGAR COOKIES

DINNER

SHRIMP CURRY WITH CONDIMENTS
OVEN RICE
BIB LETTUCE WITH ORANGE VINAIGRETTE

DESSERT

SWEDISH CREME AND FRESH FRUIT

MARTY'S OMELETS

Serves 4

Makes 4 individual omelets to your guests' liking!

8 eggs
¼ cup milk
4 drops tabasco sauce
5 T. butter or margarine
1 med. onion, chopped
1 med. green pepper,
**   chopped**
½ cup salami, chopped
½ cup shredded cheddar

1. Beat eggs and milk lightly. Add tabasco.
2. Melt 1 T. butter.
3. Saute onions, green pepper and salami for 2 minutes and set aside.
4. Melt 1 T. butter in frying pan over med./high heat. Add ¼ of the egg mixture to pan. Lift edges of egg and let uncooked egg flow under until top is almost set.
5. Spread ¼ of vegetable/salami mixture on top and finish cooking the omelet.
6. Sprinkle cheese on top. Slide on plate and fold over. Season with salt and pepper if desired.
7. Repeat steps 4 through 6 for the other 3 omelets.

You can also use chopped broccoli, turkey cubes and cream cheese as filling or any other chopped vegetable with fried, chopped bacon.

HERBAL PASTA SALAD

Serves 4

Don't be fooled by the word salad, this is served warm!

1 12 oz. box curly pasta,
  (tri-colored)
2 lg. carrots
1 med. zucchini
2 garlic cloves, minced
2 T. butter or margarine
1 T. lemon juice
3 lg. basil leaves, chopped
OR 1 t. dried basil
4 T. grated Parmesan
  cheese

1. Cook pasta according to directions on package.
2. Cut carrots and zucchini into julienne strips.
3. Melt butter in frying pan and saute vegetables and garlic until tender but crisp. Appr. 4 - 5 min.
4. Add lemon juice, basil, salt and pepper.
5. Add pasta, toss gently and heat.
6. Sprinkle with Parmesan and serve at once.
7. Place pasta salad on individual serving plates and garnish with sliced tomatoes.

SUGAR COOKIES

Yields appr. 30 cookies

1 cup shortening
  (part butter)
1 cup sugar
1 egg
1 t. vanilla
½ t. baking soda
½ t. salt
½ t. cream of tartar
2 cups flour

1. Cream shortening and sugar. Add egg and vanilla.
2. Beat mixture and add sifted dry ingredients. Roll dough into walnut size balls.
3. Flatten on baking sheets with bottom of glass dipped into sugar.
4. Bake at 350 degrees until lightly brown for 6 - 8 minutes.

Keeps guests and kids happy!

CURRIED SHRIMP WITH CONDIMENTS

Serves 4

1½ lbs. raw shrimp
3 T. butter or margarine
⅓ cup onion, chopped
3 T. flour
3 t. curry powder
¾ t. ginger
¾ t. salt
1½ cups shrimp stock
Few red pepper flakes
¾ cup milk
1½ T. lemon juice

1. Clean and devein shrimp.
2. Cover shrimp with 1½ cups of water in heavy sauce pan. Bring to a boil.
3. Allow to boil for 1 minute and drain. RESERVE WATER.
4. Melt butter in heavy skillet.
5. Saute onion until tender.
6. Add flour, curry, ginger and salt. Blend and cook over med. heat for 1 min.
7. Measure reserved shrimp stock and if necessary boil and reduce to 1½ cups. Add 1½ cups stock to mixture in skillet. Heat and stir until thickened, about 1 minute.
8. Add shrimp, milk and red pepper flakes. Heat through.
9. Add lemon juice and serve over white rice with several of the following condiments.

CONDIMENTS: *Mango chutney (a must!), chopped hard boiled egg, chopped scallions, chopped unsalted peanuts, raisins or currants, grated coconut.*

OVEN RICE

2 cups boiling water
1 T. butter or margarine
1 cup long grain rice

1. Pour boiling water into 1½ qt. casserole.
2. Stir butter in water until melted. Add rice and salt and stir.
3. Bake in 350 degree oven for 35 minutes or until rice is tender.
4. Fluff with fork after 15 minutes.

BIB LETTUCE WITH ORANGE VINAIGRETTE DRESSING

2 lg. bib lettuce
1 lg. navel orange

1. Wash and dry lettuce.
2. Peel, section and skin orange. Cut into small pieces.
3. Arrange lettuce leaves on individual salad plates and sprinkle with orange pieces.

ORANGE VINAIGRETTE
¼ cup fresh orange juice
1 T. red wine vinegar
1 t. Dijon mustard
½ cup mild olive oil
Salt and pepper to taste

1. Mix orange juice and vinegar. Whisk until blended.
2. Whisk in mustard.
3. **Very slowly** whisk in the olive oil and continue to whisk until slightly thickened.
4. Season with salt and pepper to taste.
5. Drizzle over salad before serving.

DESSERT

SWEDISH CREME AND FRESH FRUIT

Serves 4

2 cups whipping cream
1 cup sugar
1 envelope gelatin
½ pint sour cream
1 t. vanilla
½ t. almond extract

1. Mix whipping cream, sugar and gelatin.
2. Heat gently and stir until gelatin is dissolved, about 10 minutes.
3. Cool until slightly thickened.
4. Fold in sour cream. Add vanilla and almond extract and whisk. As you stir, it will get smooth and will thicken. Refrigerate!
5. Serve with fresh fruit.

Place bowl with Swedish creme in the center of a large dessert tray and arrange fresh fruit around it for dipping.

GROCERY LIST

The Accidental Hostess is well aware that one of the most tedious parts of keeping hungry guests happy is making out a GROCERY LIST. (And if you're like us, you inevitably run out and leave the irksome little devil on the kitchen counter - luckily Sanibel is small enough that, with any luck at all, you'll run into a friend who will let you borrow hers!)

But, as we said before, we're here to help any way we can. So, with your convenience and our menus in mind, we've made a list for you. The following list includes all the items needed for all the recipes on days 4 and 8. And better yet, they all can be purchased well in advance of your company's arrival. Keep these items on hand, and you stand ever ready to slam out some fairly fabulous feeds at a moments notice. It's not just easy, it's a veritable no-brainer!

SHOPPING LIST FOR DAYS 4 AND 8

DAIRY
eggs
plain non-fat yogurt
grated parmesan cheese
milk
margarine

MEAT
8 half chicken breasts
1 lb. pork tenderloin

VEGETABLES
1 lg. zucchini
1 red pepper
2 yellow squash
¼ lb. snow peas
carrots
potatoes
parsley
garlic
onions

FRUIT
4 grapefruit
4 apples
3 cups berries in season
    (or 1 pkg. frozen berries)
1 lemon

CANNED FOOD
lite mayonnaise
4 oz. jar pimientos
2½ oz. sliced black olives
8 oz. can Coco Lopez Cream of
    Coconut
15 oz. can cherry pie filling

BREADS
4 croissants
sour dough rolls

DRY GOODS

sugar
brown sugar
baking powder
baking soda
flour
grated coconut
3.5 oz. box chocolate pudding
   mix NOT instant
1 box plain chocolate cake mix
12 oz. pkg. chocolate chips
long grain rice
12 oz. pkg. curly pasta

FROZEN FOOD

16 oz. bag mixed vegetables
1 box frozen peas
pound cake

SPICES

dry mustard
vanilla
cinnamon
salt
pepper
sesame seeds
chives
thyme
paprika

MISCELLANEOUS

salad oil
red wine vinegar
soy sauce
Dijon mustard
yellow raisins
walnuts
fruit jam

SPECIAL OCCASION MENUS AND RECIPES

PICNIC ON THE BEACH

PITA POCKETS

CHIPS

NANNIE'S CHOCOLATE CHIP COOKIES

FRUIT-A-BOBS

PITA POCKETS

4 lg. pita breads
1 lg. cucumber, chopped
¼ cup red onion, chopped
½ lb. bacon, diced and fried
2 cups chopped iceberg
   lettuce
Ranch dressing

1. Cut pita breads in half.
2. Mix all other ingredients except Ranch dressing.
3. Line pita pockets with chopped lettuce.
4. Fill pita pockets with bacon mixture.
5. Pass the dressing.

Mix the ingredients at the beach, so the bacon remains crunchy. It's a refreshing and delicious sandwich!

NANNIE'S CHOCOLATE CHIP COOKIES

2½ cups flour
1 t. baking soda
1 cup butter
¼ cup sugar
¾ cup light brown sugar
1 t. vanilla
1 3½ oz. pkg. instant vanilla
   pudding (you may
   substitute butterscotch)
2 eggs
1 12 oz. pkg. chocolate chips

1. Mix flour and baking soda.
2. Combine butter, sugars, vanilla and instant pudding mix.
3. Beat in eggs.
4. Add flour mixture and chocolate chips.
5. Drop with teaspoon on ungreased cookie sheet.
6. Bake at 375 degrees for 5 - 10 minutes.

Keep these in the freezer (if you can keep your hands out of them!). These are great to keep on hand to pass at lunch or hungry times!

FRUIT-A-BOBS

⅛ cup lemon juice
⅛ cup orange juice
¾ t. sugar
1 cup fresh strawberries
1 cup seedless grapes
1 banana, cut in ¾" pieces
1 cup cantaloupe balls
8 small skewers

1. In medium bowl combine all ingredients and chill for 2 hours or more.
2. Alternate fruit on skewers
3. Serve with lemon dip, if desired.

LEMON DIP
4 oz. plain yogurt
1½ t. powdered sugar
¼ t. grated lemon peel

1. Combine all ingredients and serve with fruit.

Be sure to pack fruit-a-bobs in airtight container in the cooler!

CHECKLIST FOR PICNIC ON THE BEACH

Suntan lotion, sun block, radio, paper plates, cups, napkins (finger tip terry cloth towels work great), bowl to mix the pita bread filling, serving spoon, salt and pepper, table cloth, beach towels, garbage bags, potato chips.

COOLER I
Airtight containers for chopped cucumber, onion, bacon, lettuce, fruit-a-bobs and chocolate chip cookies. Ranch dressing and lemon dip. Lots of ice.

COOLER II
Drinks on ice

A DAY ON THE WATER

PEEL AND EAT SHRIMP

FRENCH BREAD

ASSORTED CHEESES

MARINATED VEGETABLES

KEY LIME SQUARES

PEEL AND EAT SHRIMP WITH COCKTAIL SAUCE

Serves 4

2 lbs. medium shrimp
Crab or shrimp seasoning
  (optional)

1. Place shrimp in large pot or dutch oven.
2. Cover with water and crab or shrimp seasoning, if desired.
3. Bring to a boil.
4. Remove from heat, cover and let set for 5 min.
5. Drain and chill.

COCKTAIL SAUCE
¾ cup Chili sauce
1 - 2 T. horseradish
1 t. lemon juice

1. Mix Chili sauce, horseradish and lemon juice together to make cocktail sauce.
2. Chill and serve with shrimp.

Keep shrimp and sauce well chilled or on ice. Guests peel their own. It's fun and saves you a lot of work.

MARINATED VEGETABLES

Serves 4

1 cup broccoli flowerets
1 cup cauliflower flowerets
1 cup carrot sticks
1 cup green pepper slices
1 cup red pepper slices
2 cups cubed cheddar
  cheese
1 pkg. Good Seasons Italian
  salad dressing mix

1. Mix vegetables and cheese cubes together.
2. Make dressing according to directions.
3. Pour enough dressing over the vegetables and cheese cubes to coat well.
4. Toss lightly and chill well.
5. Store and serve in air tight container.

This is easy to make and easy to serve as finger foods.

KEY LIME SQUARES

2 cups flour
½ cup powdered sugar
1 cup margarine or butter
4 eggs
2 cups sugar
Pinch salt
2 T. flour
½ t. baking powder
⅓ cup key lime juice
⅛ t. grate key lime peel
Powdered sugar

1. Combine flour and powdered sugar.
2. Add slices of margarine and mix until smooth.
3. Press dough into bottom of a 9 x 13 inch baking pan.
4. Bake at 350 degrees for 20 - 25 minutes or until golden brown.
5. In the meantime, beat eggs at high speed with electric mixer until light in color.
6. Slowly add sugar, salt, flour, baking powder, peel and key lime juice.
7. Beat at high speed for 2 - 3 minutes.
8. Pour mixture into hot pie crust and return to oven for 20 - 25 more minutes.
9. Sprinkle at once with powdered sugar.
10. Cool and cut into bars.

These freeze well.

CHECK LIST

1. Make sure the boat you are using has enough life jackets for all members of your party.

2. Encourage everyone to wear boat shoes.

3. The seas are fickle, so dress accordingly. A sweatshirt or a wind breaker is a good idea even on a warm day.

4. Make sure all your food is packed in air tight containers on plenty of ice.

5. Bring along plenty of drinks on ice and a jug of ice water.

6. Don't forget suntan lotion and sun block, serving platter for shrimp and cheeses, paper plates, napkins, cups, eating utensils, garbage bags.

WORKOUT COOKOUT

BARBECUED BABY BACK RIBS

GRILLED CORN ON THE COB

POTATOES WITH ONIONS

COLE SLAW

GRILLED BANANAS

BARBECUED BABY BACK RIBS   Serves 4

4 lbs. baby back ribs
2 cups favorite barbecue
**   sauce**

1. Brush ribs with your favorite barbecue sauce.
2. Place on pre-heated grill and grill over medium/high heat for 20 - 30 minutes, basting and turning several times.

GRILLED CORN ON THE COB   Serves 4

4 ears of corn
4 T. butter or margarine
Salt and pepper to taste

1. Boil cleaned corn for 5 minutes. Drain and rinse.
2. Place each corn on a piece of aluminum foil, brush with butter and sprinkle with salt and pepper.
3. Wrap aluminum foil tightly around corn and place on grill over medium/high heat for 15 minutes, turning several times.

POTATOES WITH ONIONS

Serves 4

4 med. baking potatoes
2 med. onions
4 t. butter
Salt and pepper to taste

1. Cut 4 separate pieces of heavy aluminum foil, each large enough to hold one potato.
2. Slice each potato into 4 or 5 thick slices. Lay one half of each potato on a piece of foil.
3. Cut onions into ⅓″ slices and put them on top of the potato slices.
4. Top with remaining potato slices.
5. Dot with butter and sprinkle with salt and pepper. Wrap tightly in foil.
6. Bake at 400 degrees for 45 minutes or cook on the barbecue grill over medium/high heat for 35 minutes.

COLE SLAW

Serves 4

1 lb. cabbage

DRESSING
1½ T. evaporated milk
2 T. sugar
2 T. vinegar
¼ cup mayonnaise
Salt to taste

1. Chop cabbage thinly.

2. Mix all ingredients for dressing and chill.
3. Before serving add dressing to cabbage until it is moistened to your liking.

GRILLED BANANAS

Serves 4

4 bananas, very ripe
4 t. brown sugar
4 t. brandy (optional)

1. Wrap each banana in a square of tin foil. Grill over medium heat for 5 - 10 minutes until soft.
2. Remove bananas from foil and cut open the peel on the inside of the banana.
3. Sprinkle with brown sugar and brandy (optional) and gently mash with fork.
4. Serve immediately. Vanilla ice cream goes great with this treat.

Use paper everything so the clean up will be easy!

DROP DEAD GREAT DINNER FOR EIGHT

SUNSET COCKTAILS

PATE AND CHEESE PLATTER

BOTTLE OF WINE

SUPER SEAFOOD WITH PASTA

CRISP GREEN SALAD

FRENCH BREAD

PINEAPPLE AND STRAWBERRIES WITH GINGER

CHICKEN LIVER PATE

This delicious pate must be prepared at least 24 hours before serving. It will keep in the refrigerator for up to 3 days.

**1 lb. chicken livers,
   trimmed**
Milk
¼ cup raisins
5 t. dry Madeira wine
**1 stick unsalted butter,
   softened**
¼ cup Armagnac or Cognac
1 garlic clove, crushed
2 T. heavy cream
1½ t. fresh lemon juice
Dash ginger
Dash ground cloves
Dash nutmeg
Dash cinnamon
Salt and pepper to taste
Crackers

1. Separate the 2 lobes of each chicken liver and place in medium size bowl.
2. Add enough milk to cover.
3. Cover and refrigerate overnight.
4. In a small saucepan, combine raisins with 4 t. Madeira and ⅓ cup water. Bring to a boil. Remove from heat at once and set aside. Let stand until raisins are soft, about 10 - 15 minutes.
5. Drain the chicken livers and pat dry with paper towels.
6. In a lg. skillet melt 3 T. butter and cook the chicken livers over medium heat, tossing, for about 5 minutes. They should be firm but still pink on the inside. Remove from heat.
7. With a slotted spoon transfer the livers to a food processor.
8. Add Armagnac to the skillet, stir and scrape to blend it with the pan juices.
9. Pour liquid from pan to food processor. Add garlic, heavy cream, lemon juice, 1 t. Madeira, spices and 5 T. softened butter. Puree until mixture is smooth by turning the machine on and off and scraping down the sides.
10. Transfer mixture to a bowl and add the drained raisins. Season with salt and pepper to taste.
11. Transfer pate to a serving dish, cover and refrigerate for 24 hours.

Serve with water crackers, pita chips or thinly sliced toast, cut into triangles

SUPER SEAFOOD WITH PASTA   Serves 8

When you buy the shrimp, we suggest you purchase an inexpensive shrimp cleaner and ask the fish store proprietor to demonstrate its use. It makes the shrimp cleaning easy and quick.

6 T. butter or margarine
¼ t. crushed dried red pepper flakes
3 cloves garlic, finely chopped
1 lb. large shrimp, cleaned, deveined and cut in half lengthwise (16 - 20 shrimps to a lb.)
1½ lbs. sea scallops (large)
2 med. tomatoes, chopped
2 3 oz. jar capers, drained
1½ cups white wine
1 T. cornstarch
¼ cup water
16 oz. linguini pasta
½ cup parsley, chopped
Grated Parmesan cheese to taste

1. Melt butter in lg. frying pan and saute red pepper flakes and garlic for 30 seconds.
2. Add shrimp and scallops and saute until done over medium/high heat (about 2 minutes).
3. Add tomatoes and capers and cook appr. 30 seconds, just enough to heat through.
4. Add white wine and bring to a simmer.
5. Mix cornstarch and water, blending well. Add to pan. Heat until slightly thickened. Serve at once over linguini. Sprinkle with parsley and Parmesan cheese.

Experienced cooks can substitute angel hair pasta for the linguini. Follow cooking directions carefully, angel hair pasta is done very quickly. Use all shrimp or scallops, if preferred.

CRISP GREEN SALAD

Serves 8

1½ heads Romaine lettuce
3 lg. tomatoes
1 lg. avocado
1 med. red onion
Olive oil and vinegar
Salt and pepper to taste

1. Choose a pretty large platter.
2. Tear romaine into bite size pieces and lay on the platter.
3. Slice tomatoes and circle them on the lettuce.
4. Slice red onion and arrange them on platter.
5. Cube avocado and surround tomatoes and onion rings.
6. Drizzle with oil and vinegar.
7. Sprinkle salt and pepper to taste.

PINEAPPLE AND STRAWBERRIES WITH GINGER

Serves 8

1½ T. fresh ginger, grated
½ cup sugar
Juice of ½ lg. lemon
2 cups water
1 lg. pineapple, cut into bite size pieces
2 pints fresh strawberries, sliced

1. Peel and grate ginger.
2. Combine sugar, lemon and water. Bring to a boil.
3. Add ginger and simmer for 5 minutes.
4. Pour hot syrup over cut pineapple. CHILL FOR SEVERAL HOURS OR OVERNIGHT.
5. At serving time, add sliced, chilled strawberries.

This is a refreshing and light dessert. It's also a great hit at breakfast time.

AFTER THEATER DESSERT AND COFFEE

POT-AU-CHOCOLATE

SPECIAL COFFEES

POT-AU-CHOCOLATE

Serves 4 - 6

½ cup water
¼ cup sugar
1 6 oz. pkg. semi-sweet
    chocolate chips
3 egg yolks
2 cups heavy cream
2 t. Creme de Menthe OR
    brandy

1. Boil sugar and water together for 3 minutes.
2. Put syrup in blender, add chocolate chips and grind for 10 seconds.
3. Cool to room temperature.
4. Add egg yolks to mixture and blend for 10 seconds.
5. Add heavy cream and 1 t. of liqueur and blend for 20 seconds.
6. Pour into 4 to 6 serving glasses. Cover with foil and freeze.

Garnish with whipped cream, flavored with the remaining 1 t. liqueur and chocolate shavings.

SPECIAL COFFEES

If you serve these coffees in tall glasses, pour the hot coffee over a metal spoon in the glass to avoid breaking it.

CAFE DE SPECIALE
Yields 1 serving

8 oz. hot black coffee
½ oz. Coconut Rum
½ oz. Kaluha
½ oz. Cointreau
Whipped cream
Nutmeg

1. Pour hot coffee into tall 12 oz. glass.
2. Add Rum, Kaluha and Cointreau. Stir and blend.
3. Top with a swirl of whipped cream and sprinkle with nutmeg.

CAFE DE ORANGE
Yields 1 serving

1 t. brown sugar
8 oz. hot black coffee
½ oz. orange cognac brandy
½ oz. dark rum
Whipped cream

1. Place sugar in tall 12 oz. glass.
2. Add 2 oz. of the coffee. Stir until sugar has dissolved.
3. Add cognac brandy, rum and remaining coffee, mixing well.
4. Top with swirl of whipped cream.

CAFE DE MIAMI
Yields 1 serving

1 oz. coffee liqueur
½ oz. white creme de menthe
8 oz. hot black coffee
Whipped cream
1 t. semi-sweet chocolate shavings

1. Pour liqueurs into tall 12 oz. glass.
2. Add hot coffee. Stir well.
3. Top with swirl of whipped cream.
4. Sprinkle with chocolate shavings.

CINNAMON COFFEE

4 Servings

Place ground coffee into filter and add ½ t. cinnamon per 4 cups of coffee to the grinds. Prepare coffee as usual. Serve in tall glasses or cups. Garnish with a swirl of whipping cream and a few sprinkles of cinnamon on top of the whipping cream. You may also place a cinnamon stick into each cup.

VANILLA COFFEE

4 servings

Prepare coffee as usual. Add 1 t. vanilla extract per 4 cups to the hot coffee. Serve in cups or tall glasses. Garnish with whipping cream and shavings of semi-sweet chocolate.

OLD FRIENDS MEET NEW FRIENDS
COCKTAIL PARTY

SALMON MOUSSE

FRESH ASPARAGUS WITH DIP

SPICY SHRIMP

GINGER SHRIMP

ARTICHOKE SPRING LEAVES

CHEESE BALL

CHILI CON QUESO

TEX MEX SNACK

GUACAMOLE

YOGURT VEGETABLE DIP

ORANGE CRANBERRY DIP

SPINACH DIP WITH PITA BREAD CHIPS

EASY BLENDER DAIQUIRIS

SALMON MOUSSE

1 8 oz. can pink salmon,
   boneless and skinless
1 pkg. unflavored gelatin
1 lg. cucumber
1 T. lemon juice
½ t. horseradish
2 t. onion, finely grated
½ cup plain low fat yogurt
½ cup lite mayonnaise
¼ t. salt
Parsley

1. Drain salmon and reserve liquid. Add water to make ¼ cup liquid and pour into medium sauce pan.
2. Sprinkle gelatin into liquid and let stand for 5 minutes. Then stir over low heat until gelatin is dissolved.
3. Peel, seed and chop cucumber. Process briefly in blender and drain excess liquid.
4. Add lemon juice, horseradish, onion and dissolved gelatin to drained cucumber.
5. Mix yogurt with mayonnaise and blend with cucumber mixture. Add salt.
6. Spray 3 cup mold with cooking spray and pour mousse into mold. Chill at least 5 hours.
7. Before serving, dip mold briefly into hot water and unmold mousse onto serving platter.
8. Garnish with parsley.

Serve with English wafers.

FRESH ASPARAGUS WITH DIP

1 lb. fresh asparagus
½ t. baking soda
Dressing of your choice

1. Boil water in large pan.
2. Add baking soda to preserve green color.
3. Steam asparagus for 1 - 2 minutes.
4. Drain and rinse with cold water. Chill.
5. Arrange on oval serving platter and serve with Thousand Island, Russian or Ranch dressing.

Garnish with thinly sliced lemon or a fresh flower from your garden.

SPICY SHRIMP   Serves 8

1 lb. medium size fresh
  shrimp
2 T. vegetable oil
3 green onions, chopped
1 t. fresh ginger, minced
½ cup chicken broth
3 T. ketchup
2 T. cider vinegar
2 T. white wine
1 t. sugar
⅛ t. cayenne pepper
Boston lettuce

1. Shell and devein shrimp.
2. Heat 1 T vegetable oil over medium-high heat for 1 minute. Add shrimp and stir fry for 1 - 2 minutes. Transfer to bowl.
3. Add the remaining oil to skillet and heat. Add ginger and ⅔ of the green onions and stir fry for 1 minute.
4. Add chicken broth, ketchup, vinegar, wine, sugar and cayenne pepper. Simmer and stir for about 3 minutes or until sauce thickens slightly.
5. Return shrimp to skillet. Stir while cooking 2 - 3 minutes.
6. Transfer to bowl, cover and refrigerate for several hours.
7. Arrange Boston lettuce on attractive plate and mound shrimp on top. Sprinkle rest of the green onions over shrimp and serve.

GINGER SHRIMP

1 lb. medium size fresh
   shrimp
¼ cup corn oil
4 thin slices fresh ginger
1 stalk scallion
2 T. dry sherry
½ t. salt
½ t. sugar

1. With a scissor cut off the shrimps feet. Cut and open a small section of each back of shell and remove the black vein. Wash and drain shrimp. Dry throughly with paper towels.
2. Cut scallion into 2″ pieces.
3. Place wok or frying pan over medium heat for 1 - 2 minutes, until hot.
4. Add oil, ginger, scallion and shrimp, stirring over high heat for 2 - 3 minutes.
5. Add salt, sugar, sherry and cover wok.
6. Cook for 1 more minute or until the shrimp's shell starts to separate from the meat. Remove shells.
7. Place shrimp with sauce in bowl, cover and refrigerate for one hour.
8. Remove shrimp from sauce and serve on plate decorated with a hibiscus.

ARTICHOKE SPRING LEAVES   Serves 10 - 12

1 lg. artichoke
Juice of 1 lemon
½ cup mayonnaise
½ t. curry powder
8 oz. cooked small shrimp

1. Cut off stem with scissor. Trim the top leaves by one-fourth. Remove the bottom row of leaves. Dip the trimmed base in lemon juice to avoid discoloration.
2. Place the artichoke top down on a trivet over 1 or 2 inches boiling water and steam for about 45 min. or until tender.
3. Drain and refrigerate.
4. Mix mayonnaise with curry.
5. Peel off artichoke leaves and put a dab of mixture on the meaty end of each artichoke leaf.
6. Place one shrimp on top of the mayonnaise.
7. Arrange on platter in a sunburst pattern.

Can be prepared early in the day and assembled shortly before serving.

CHEESE BALL   Yields 1

Must be prepared one day before serving.

1 8 oz. pkg. cream cheese
2 5 oz. glasses Borden's
   English Sharp Cheddar
1 5 oz. glass Roka Blue
   Cheese
2 T. chopped onion
½ t. Accent
1 cup ground pecans
½ cup parsley flakes

1. Mix ingredients together reserving ½ cup nuts and ¼ cup parsley.
2. Refrigerate overnight.
3. Next day roll cheese mixture into ball and roll in reserved nuts and parsley.
4. Serve with crackers.

The cheese ball can be made ahead of time and kept frozen for up to one year.

CHILI CON QUESO

1½ lbs. Velveeta cheese
1 10 oz. can Rotel whole
   tomatoes and green
   chilies

1. Melt cheese. Add tomatoes and chilies.
2. Heat thoroughly and serve at once.

Serve with corn chips or tortilla chips.

TEX-MEX-SNACK

1 lb. hamburger meat
1 med. onion, chopped
1 med. green pepper,
   chopped
1 pkg. Taco seasoning mix
1 8 oz. can tomato sauce
1 16 oz. can refried beans
1 cup cheddar cheese,
   grated

1. In large frying pan brown meat and saute onion and green pepper. Drain fat.
2. Add seasoning mix, tomato sauce and mix well.
3. Stir in beans and pour into oven proof serving dish.
4. Top with cheese and heat in oven until cheese has melted.

Serve with fritas or tortillas. It's a hearty appetizer!

GUACAMOLE

Yields about 1¾ cups

2 lg. avocados, ripe
3 T. lemon juice
4 canned green chilies
½ t. salt
2 t. minced cilantro OR
½ t. coriander
2 green onions
1 clove garlic
1 lg. tomato
Dash of tabasco
Corn chips

1. Cut avocado in half, reserve pit. Peel and mash coarsely with a fork while blending in the lemon juice.
2. Seed and chop the chilies.
3. Finely chop onions and garlic.
4. Peel and chop the tomato.
5. Add all but tomato and blend well.
6. Fold in tomato.
7. Place avocado pit in center until serving time to prevent discoloration.
8. Serve with corn chips.

If the avocados aren't ripe enough, wrap them in newspaper and place them in your cupboard until ripe.

YOGURT VEGETABLE DIP

Yields 2 cups

1 8 oz. pkg. cream cheese, cubed and softened
1 pkg. ranch style dressing mix
1 T. milk
1 cup low fat yogurt

1. In blender beat cream cheese, dressing mix and milk until smooth.
2. Add yogurt and blend well.
3. Cover and chill until serving time.

Serve with cut vegetables. Try using half a cleaned green pepper as a serving dish for this dip.

ORANGE CRANBERRY DIP

Yields 1¼ cups

1 cup low fat yogurt
½ cup cranberry-orange
    relish
¼ t. ground ginger
¼ t. ground nutmeg
1 large apple
1 navel orange
1 cup fresh pineapple
    chunks
2 cups seedless green
    grapes

1. Mix yogurt, cranberry relish, nutmeg and ginger.
2. Cover and chill until serving time.
3. Just before serving, core and slice apple.
4. Peel and section orange.
5. Core and chunk pineapple.

Serve dip with fresh fruit.

SPINACH DIP WITH PITA BREAD CHIPS

1 4 oz. can water chestnuts
1 green onion
1 pkg. frozen spinach
¾ cup sour cream
½ cup mayonnaise
½ pkg. vegetable soup mix

1. Drain water chestnuts and chop. Chop onion. Thaw and squeeze the water out of spinach.
2. Put remaining ingredients in a food processor. Blend until smooth. Stir in spinach, water chestnuts and onion. Pour into bowl.

PITA BREAD CHIPS

8 lg. pita bread pockets
    (whole wheat or onion)
Melted butter
Garlic salt
Parmesan cheese

1. Preheat oven to 350 degrees.
2. Split pita in half and brush inside lightly with melted butter.
3. Sprinkle with garlic salt and Parmesan cheese.
4. Bake until crisp, about 15 minutes.

EASY BLENDER DAIQUIRIS

Double this recipe to serve 8 by mixing two batches of daiquiris.

1 6 oz. can frozen limeade
6 oz. light rum
Crushed ice
Fresh lime slices

1. Pour frozen limeade into blender.
2. Add 1 can (6 oz.) rum.
3. Fill blender with crushed ice.
4. Blend until well mixed.
5. Serve in stemmed glass garnished with a lime slice.

If you prefer a light green color, add 2 - 3 drops light green food coloring.

RECIPES FOR SPRING BREAKERS OR LARGE GROUPS

CHILI OVER PASTA

APRICOT CHICKEN

EASY LASAGNA

SEAFOOD CHOWDER

SLOPPY JOES

BAKED BEANS

BAKED VEGETABLES

COLE SLAW

GRANDMA CHURCH'S CHOCOLATE CHIP CAKE

MINT ICE CREAM PIE

UNBEATABLE BROWNIES

CHILI OVER PASTA

Serves 10

2 lbs. lean ground beef
3 - 4 green onions
1 t. chili powder
1 t. cayenne
1 t. cumin
1 t. cinnamon
1 t. garlic salt
2 T. parsley, chopped
1 t. black pepper
1 square baking chocolate
1 29 oz. can tomato sauce
1 16 oz. can Hunts Tomato
  Sauce Special
1 15 oz. can kidney beans
2 lbs. pasta

1. Saute meat and onions.
2. Add all seasoning and blend.
3. Add the chocolate and blend.
4. Add tomato sauces and one 29 oz. can of water.
5. Simmer for 30 minutes.
6. Add beans and simmer for 5 more minutes.
7. Cook pasta according to directions.
8. Serve chili over pasta.

Top with shredded cheddar cheese, chopped yellow onion, jalopeno peppers. If you like it very hot, add some hot sauce.

APRICOT CHICKEN

Serves 12

3 three lb. frying chickens, quartered
1 12 oz. jar apricot preserves
1 8 oz. bottle Russian salad dressing
1 pkg. dried French onion soup mix

1. Remove extra fat and skin from chicken. Place in baking dishes. Bake at 350 degrees for 30 min.
2. Mix apricot preserves, Russian dressing and onion soup mix into sauce.
3. Pour over chicken. Continue cooking for 30 more minutes, basting often.

This has a delightfully different flavor.

EASY LASAGNA

2 lbs. Italian sausage
2 28 oz. jars favorite
   spaghetti sauce
1 16 oz. pkg. lasagna
   noodles
1 lb. Ricotta cheese
1 egg, whisked
1 T parsley, chopped
12 oz. shredded Mozzarella
   cheese
1 cup grated Parmesan
   cheese

1. Brown sausage in a hot skillet. Add ¼ cup water cover and simmer 15 min. Drain and chop into small pieces.
2. Add to spaghetti sauce. Simmer 15 min. to blend flavors.
3. Cook lasagna noodles according to package directions. Drain and wash with cold water.
4. Mix Ricotta, whisked egg and parsley together.
5. Place about 1 cup sauce on bottom of 13 x 9 x 2 casserole dish.
6. Layer remaining ingredients as follows:
   Noodles
   Sauce
   Ricotta mixture
   Mozzarella
   Parmesan

You'll get four layers ending with cheeses.

At this point it can be:

1. Baked at 350 degrees for 35 minutes.
2. Refrigerated for up to 24 hours.
3. Frozen for up to 3 months.

If refrigerated or frozen, allow to return to room temperature before baking at 350 degrees for 35 minutes.

If there is any sauce left, heat and pass with the lasagna.

Serve this with garlic bread and a green salad for an inexpensive crowd pleaser which can be prepared well in advance.

SEAFOOD CHOWDER

Serves 12

This is a great way to use your guests' catch of the day or left over frozen fish.

6 T. butter
4 med. onions, chopped
1 green pepper, chopped
1 cup celery, chopped
2 cloves garlic, minced
3 T. flour
2 30 oz. cans stewed
   tomatoes
1 64 oz. can V-8 or clamato
   juice
2 t. salt
4 t. sugar
8 bay leaves
2 t. thyme
1 t. allspice
6 T. Worcestershire sauce
½ t. hot pepper sauce
2 7 oz. cans tuna, drained
2 7 oz. cans shrimp,
   undrained
2 6 oz. bottles clam juice
2 lbs. fresh or frozen fish,
   any kind
½ cup sherry, warmed
   (optional)

1. Melt butter. Add onions, pepper, celery and garlic. Saute until tender.
2. Blend in flour.
3. Add tomatoes, V-8 or clamato juice, salt, sugar, bay leaves, thyme, allspice, Worcestershire sauce and hot pepper sauce.
4. Simmer 15 minutes.
5. Add tuna, shrimp, clams, clam juice and fish that has been cut into bite size pieces.
6. Simmer 15 more minutes.
7. If desired, top with warm sherry.

This is great on a cool evening served with loaves of crunchy French bread. Freeze leftovers for later.

SLOPPY JOES
Serves 16

3 lbs. ground beef
3 10¾ oz. cans chicken
   gumbo soup
1½ cups ketchup
¾ cup brown sugar
16 hamburger buns

1. Brown meat in skillet. Drain fat.
2. Add soup and stir.
3. Add ketsup and brown sugar. Stir well.
4. Heat covered over medium for 15 minutes.
5. Serve on hamburger buns.

Serve this with chips and our favorite green vegetable - a pickle - they'll love it!

BAKED BEANS
Serves 12

2 32 oz. cans baked beans
1½ cups ketchup
1½ cups sugar
1 t. cinnamon
1 t. allspice
Nutmeg to taste
1½ cups onions, chopped
2 cups corn flakes
½ lb. bacon

1. Mix first seven ingredients and pour into baking dish.
2. Top with corn flakes and raw bacon strips.
3. Bake ½ hour at 350 degrees.

These taste great with hot dogs and hamburgers!

BAKED VEGETABLES

Serves 8

1 16 oz. bag frozen yellow
   corn
3 med. zucchini, sliced
3 med. tomatoes, cut into
   small wedges
2 med. onions, cut into small
   wedges
2 med. green pepper, cut
   into 1" squares
2 t. Italian seasoning
¼ cup bread crumbs
¼ cup Parmesan cheese
   desired degree of

1. Mix cleaned and sliced vegetables together in a large baking dish.
2. Sprinkle vegetables with Italian seasoning and mix well.
3. Dot with butter or margarine.
4. Bake for 15 minutes in 400 degree oven.
5. Sprinkle with bread crumbs and Parmesan cheese.
6. Continue to bake for another 5 minutes or until desired degree of doneness. Do not overcook.

COLE SLAW

Serves 10 or more

5 lbs. cabbage

DRESSING
$1/3$ cup evaporated milk
¾ cup sugar
$1/3$ t salt
¼ cup vinegar
1 cup mayonnaise

1. Chop cabbage thinly.
2. Mix all ingredients for dressing and chill.
3. Before serving add dressing to cabbage until it is moistened to your liking.

GRANDMA CHURCH'S CHOCOLATE CHIP CAKE

Serves 12

1 3½ oz. pkg. chocolate
   pudding mix (not
   instant)
1 box chocolate cake mix
1 6 oz. pkg. chocolate chips

1. Prepare chocolate pudding according to directions on package and let cool.
2. Add the cake mix and stir.
3. Transfer mixture to a greased 9 x 13 baking pan.
4. Sprinkle with chocolate chips and bake in preheated oven at 350 degrees for 25 - 30 minutes.

Grandma Church's kids loved this and yours will love it too!

MINT ICE CREAM PIE

4 sq. unsweetened
  chocolate
2 sticks (½ lb) butter or
  margarine
1½ cups sugar
4½ cups Coco Krispies
  cereal
½ gal. mint chocolate chip
  ice cream

1. Melt butter and chocolate together.
2. Mix in sugar and cereal.
3. Grease 2 9″ pie tins or 1 large rectangular pan.
4. Turn chocolate mixture into tins and pat into place.
5. Freeze briefly to set (about 15 min.).
6. Soften ice cream and spread on top of chocolate crust mixture.
7. Freeze until serving time.

This is GREAT! A major kid pleaser and couldn't be easier to prepare.

UNBEATABLE BROWNIES

Yields 3 dozen

4 eggs
2 cups sugar
1 cup unsalted butter,
  melted
3 1 oz. squares
  unsweetened chocolate,
  melted
2 t. vanilla
1½ cups flour
1 t. baking powder
1 t. salt
1 cup chopped walnuts,
  optional

1. Beat together eggs, sugar, butter and chocolate.
2. Add vanilla, flour, baking powder and salt, mixing after each addition.
3. Stir in nuts, if desired.
4. Pour into a greased and floured 9 x 13 pan. Bake at 350 degrees for 30 min.
5. Let cool for 45 minutes before cutting.

As easy as a mix!

INDEX

CAKES, COOKIES AND PIES

FRUIT AND OTHER DESSERTS

MEATS AND POULTRY

PASTA

POTATOES

RICE

SALADS - DINNER

SALAD DRESSINGS

SALADS - LUNCH
Apple Tuna Salad, 49
Caesar Salad, 72
Chinese Chicken Salad, 78
Ginger Fruit Salad, 89
Herbal Pasta Salad, 95
Moni's Chicken Salad a la Peach, 67
Sauteed Chicken Salad, 42
Seafood Salad, 56
Vegetable Pasta Salad, 62

SAUCES
Apricot Glaze, 84
Lemon Dip, 104
Mustard Sauce, 84
Shrimp Cocktail Sauce, 106
Tartar Sauce, 44

SEAFOOD
Florida Fried Fish, 44
Grilled Sword Fish, 68
Mary's Baked Fish, 79
Peel and Eat Shrimp, 106
Shrimp Curry, 96
Super Seafood with Pasta, 114

SOUPS
Gazpacho, 49
Seafood Chowder, 132

VEGETABLES
Baked Beans, 133
Baked Tomatoes, 58
Baked Vegetables, 134
Broccoli in Orange Sauce, 80
Cauliflower Scramble, 74
Corn on the Cob, Grilled, 109
Green Beans with Dill, 52
Marinated Vegetables, 106
Snow Peas and Carrots, 64
Steamed Broccoli, 45
Stir Fried Vegetables, 85
Vegetable Fritata, 83

ORDER FORM

DO YOU KNOW OF ANYONE ELSE WHO MIGHT ENJOY **THE ACCIDENTAL HOSTESS?** EXTRA COPIES CAN BE OBTAINED BY COMPLETING THE FORM BELOW.

PLEASE ENCLOSE YOUR CHECK OR MONEY ORDER MADE PAYABLE TO: THE ACCIDENTAL HOSTESS, INC.

SHIP TO:

NAME: _____

ADDRESS: _____

_____

TEL. NO.: _____

NO. OF BOOKS $9.95 EACH   TOTAL _____

_____ _____

6% FLORIDA SALES TAX _____ _____

SHIPPING & HANDLING $2.00 EACH _____ _____

                    TOTAL ENCLOSED _____

PLEASE DO NOT MAIL CASH! CHECK OR MONEY ORDER ONLY.

THE ACCIDENTAL HOSTESS, INC.
P. O. BOX 1503
SANIBEL ISLAND, FLORIDA 33957

ORDER FORM

DO YOU KNOW OF ANYONE ELSE WHO MIGHT ENJOY **THE ACCIDENTAL HOSTESS?** EXTRA COPIES CAN BE OBTAINED BY COMPLETING THE FORM BELOW.

PLEASE ENCLOSE YOUR CHECK OR MONEY ORDER MADE PAYABLE TO: THE ACCIDENTAL HOSTESS, INC.

SHIP TO:

NAME: _____

ADDRESS: _____

_____

TEL. NO.: _____

NO. OF BOOKS _____ $9.95 EACH   TOTAL   _____

_____   _____

6% FLORIDA SALES TAX _____   _____

SHIPPING & HANDLING $2.00 EACH _____   _____

TOTAL ENCLOSED _____   _____

PLEASE DO NOT MAIL CASH! CHECK OR MONEY ORDER ONLY.

THE ACCIDENTAL HOSTESS, INC.
P. O. BOX 1503
SANIBEL ISLAND, FLORIDA 33957